SOUTHERN WHITE PROTESTANTISM
in the Twentieth Century

SOUTHERN WHITE PROTESTANTISM

in the Twentieth Century

Kenneth K. Bailey

HARPER & ROW, PUBLISHERS

NEW YORK, EVANSTON, AND LONDON

Grateful acknowledgment is made to the American Historical Association, Inc., for permission to reprint Chapter 1, "Southern White Protestantism at the Turn of the Century," from American Historical Review, LXVIII *(April, 1963), pages 618–635.*

FIRST EDITION

LIBRARY OF CONGRESS CATALOG CARD NUMBER: 64–19493

G-O

To Māry

Contents

PREFACE

Of all major sections of the United States, the South conforms least to those traits and conditions normally ascribed to our national character. Slavery marked it as a region apart before 1865, and the Civil War left its heavy imprint on virtually all institutions. Memories of the Lost Cause die slowly even now. Success, wealth, and riches have been less a hope and less a reality in the South than in the North. The growth of industry was retarded, and southern agriculture languished for many years under a multitude of handicaps and adversities—technological backwardness, soil erosion, overproduction, the boll weevil, share crop tenancy, usurious furnishing merchants, and the crop lien system, to name a few. In politics, issues and alternatives have been peculiarly obscured by the notion—now rapidly waning —that a good southerner is always and inexorably a good Democrat. In race relations, the region is of course distinguished by the fervor with which white supremacy has been maintained.

Yet it is perhaps in the sphere of religion that the southern identity is best delineated. Protestantism reigns supreme in the South to an extent unmatched in this hemisphere. Nowhere else, almost surely, is there a Protestant population of equal size so renowned for its piety or for its commitment to old-fashioned Scriptural literalism. The Southern Baptists, Methodists, and Presbyterians continued as sectional denominations through the first third of this century, and the Baptists and Presbyterians remain so now. And it is with these three bodies that this study is primarily concerned. My chief effort is to survey their responses to challenges in this century, and to portray them in interaction with their culture.

I am particularly indebted to several friends, each of whom has read and offered valuable suggestions on one or more chapters: Professors Henry L. Swint and Dewey W. Grantham of Vanderbilt University, Professors Samuel S. Hill, Jr., and Robert Moats Miller of the University of North Carolina, Professors Merton L. Dillon and Thomas G. Manning of Texas Technological College, Professors Robert N. Burlingame, Wayne E. Fuller, and Ralph L. Lowenstein of Texas Western College, Professor William T. Hagan of North Texas State University, Professor T. Harry Williams of Louisiana State University, and Professor C. Leonard Lundin of Indiana University. They have saved me from many errors of fact and abominations of style. But their counsel was not heeded in all matters, and they must not be blamed for the flaws that remain. Mrs. Winifred M. Middagh rendered valuable assistance as a typist and proofreader, and Mrs. Virginia C. Persman in the preparation of the index. Mrs. Leslie Puryear and Mrs. Betty W. Swint performed expertly as research assistants in Nashville, Tennessee, in the final preparation of the manuscript.

I am also deeply indebted to the staffs and librarians of the Dargan-Carver Library, official repository of the Historical Commission of the Southern Baptist Convention, the Methodist Publishing House Library, and the Joint University Libraries—all in Nashville, Tennessee—the Historical Foundation of the Presbyterian Church in the United States, Montreat, North Carolina, the library of the Southern Baptist Theological Seminary, Louisville, Kentucky, and the Louisiana State University Library, Baton Rouge, Louisiana.

Financial assistance was provided by a Social Science Research Council grant-in-aid, and by faculty research grants from Louisiana State University and Texas Western College.

El Paso, Texas   Kenneth K. Bailey
April 1, 1964

SOUTHERN WHITE PROTESTANTISM
in the Twentieth Century

1

SOUTHERN WHITE PROTESTANTISM AT THE TURN OF THE CENTURY

*D*uring the last dreary days of the Confederacy, a Mississippi Methodist preacher defiantly exhorted his people: "If we cannot gain our *political*, let us establish at least our *mental* independence."[1] The preacher's plea was portentous, for the future would demonstrate that military conquest had exacted no spiritual surrender. A proud and undaunted *"mental* independence" survived and flourished among southerners—a fountain both of weakness and of strength, of cohesion and of strife.[2]

---

[1] The Reverend Robert H. Crozier of Sardis, Mississippi, wrote his exhortation in May 1865 and published it in the preface of his novel *The Confederate Spy: A History of the War of 1861* (Gallatin, Tenn., 1866), 5–6. This chapter was published substantially as it appears here in the *American Historical Review*, LXVIII (Apr. 1963), 618–35.

[2] Three able treatments of the southern identity are: C. Vann Woodward, *The Burden of Southern History* (Baton Rouge, 1960); Francis B. Simkins, "The South," in *Regionalism in America*, ed. Merrill Jensen (Madison, Wis.,

It was in the ranks of southern Protestantism, however, that separatism thrived most conspicuously. Forty years after Appomattox, 3,500,000 of 6,200,000 white church members in the South still belonged to three explicitly southern denominations: Southern Baptist, the Methodist Episcopal Church, South, and the (Southern) Presbyterian Church in the United States.[3] Most others held membership in locally independent congregations unaffiliated with episcopate, presbytery, conference, or convention. Indeed, except in a few urban districts and in the Catholic areas of Louisiana, Texas, and Kentucky, extraregional ecclesiastical ties were almost absent.[4] The numerically weak Episcopal and Lutheran churches were exceptions. Nor was the cleavage less apparent in content and emphasis. A New England clergyman marveled in 1900 that "one could not sit in the assembly hall of a Southern [Baptist] Convention fifteen minutes without being thoroughly convinced that he was not north of the Mason and Dixon Line";[5] another northerner was "simply forced to the conclusion" that the "Northern mind is more given to skepticism than the Southern."[6] A southerner observed that "the leaders of the Southern churches, having considered the matter, have been convinced that the religion existing among the whites of the South was of a purer form than that existing in the North."[7]

Fierce sectarian debate often obscured a consensus on fun-

1954), 147–72; and "The Status and Future of Regionalism—A Symposium," *Journal of Southern History*, XXVI (Feb. 1960), 22–56.

[3] In Oklahoma, Kentucky, and the eleven states of the former Confederacy; this included 1,820,281 Southern Baptists, 1,443,517 Southern Methodists, and approximately 230,000 Southern Presbyterians. (US Department of Commerce and Labor, Bureau of the Census, *Religious Bodies: 1906* [2 pts., Washington, D. C., 1910], I, 542–63.)

[4] *Ibid.*; 1,120,045 out of 1,398,676 southern Catholics lived in Louisiana, Texas, and Kentucky.

[5] Frank Dixon, "Southern Baptists through Northern Eyes," in Macon, Georgia, *Christian Index*, June 28, 1900.

[6] "Skepticism in the North," in Louisville *Western Recorder*, Dec. 15, 1898.

[7] James C. Hinton, "Educational Problems in the South," *Quarterly Review of the Methodist Episcopal Church, South*, V (Oct. 1883), 697.

damentals. On such concepts as heaven and hell, God
Satan, depravity and redemption, there was little dis[
Few southerners doubted the literal authenticity of
Scriptures or the ever-presence of God in man's affairs.[8] Pon-
dering a yellow fever epidemic in 1879, the Southern Baptist
Convention appointed a Special Committee on the Fearful
Scourge and adopted a report declaring in part:

How far this has been intended of God as a "terrible scourge"
upon our land, we cannot attempt to say. Secret things belong unto
God, and in time, no doubt, he will be his own interpreter. At the
present we can only say:

> God moves in a mysterious way
> His wonders to perform.

And in humility we must bow our heads and our hearts, and sub-
mit to His will, who doeth all things well.[9]

In 1905 a committee of the Southern Presbyterian General
Assembly attributed a series of railway accidents to the operation of trains on Sunday. "So long as the nation shows such
utter disregard for His authority," the committee declared,
"so long may we expect the continued repetition of these
and other so-called accidents." The Dallas *Baptist Herald*
conjectured that the San Francisco earthquake of 1906 was
designed to "shock us into attention to his words that life is
but a span and that eternity is all in all."[10] It was an outlook
handed down from an earlier, more primitive environment,
and its continuing prevalence mirrored a general intransigence.

---

[8] "In spite of considerable ecclesiastical differences the theology of the South
is the same in its broad essentials among all the religious groups. Whether one
meets in a Quaker Meeting House in Guilford County, North Carolina, or a
Methodist Church in Savannah, or in St. Louis Cathedral in New Orleans, the
basal religious philosophy is the same. Scratch any sectarian back and the same
orthodox blood flows." (Edwin McNeill Poteat, Jr., "Religion in the South,"
in *Culture in the South*, ed. W. T. Couch [Chapel Hill, 1934], 261.)

[9] Southern Baptist Convention, *Proceedings, 1879* (Atlanta, 1879), 41.

[10] Presbyterian Church in the United States, General Assembly, *Minutes,
1905* (Richmond, Va., 1905), 98. Dallas *Baptist Herald*, Apr. 26, 1906.

The rural homogeneity of the South was little disturbed by immigration, industrialization, new intellectual currents, and all those other forces which were elsewhere transforming society. As in politics the ascendancy of the Democratic party seldom was challenged, so in religion orthodoxy reigned supreme. Doubters and village atheists were few.[11]

Ecclesiastical isolation fostered intraregional accommodations between church and society. Thus, in the late nineteenth century, as racial distinctions in secular spheres were being drawn more sharply, southern Protestants busily regrouped into all-white and all-Negro denominations. Perhaps the separation resulted less from design than unplanned evolution, but it was happily observed in many quarters. As early as February 1866 a contributor to the Macon, Georgia, *Christian Index* predicted that "their [Negro] separation from the white churches is only a question of time"; later that year Negro Baptist congregations in South Carolina, Georgia, and Florida organized an all-Negro Zion Association. The white Shelby County, Alabama, Baptist Association refused to receive messengers from a Negro Baptist church in 1867, and afterward advised the congregation to "wait until opportunity is afforded them of forming colored associations." In 1869 the South Carolina State Baptist Convention sanctioned "the separate organization into churches, associations and Sabbath schools of our colored brethren, when such separate organization may be desired." In 1872, for the first time, the Sunday School Board of the Southern Baptist Convention explicitly excluded Negro congregations from its semiofficial statistical compila-

[11] During the famous Scopes trial at Dayton, Tennessee, in 1925, Henry L. Mencken found no local resident who doubted "so much as the typographical errors in Holy Writ." "To call a man a doubter in these parts," he averred, "is equal to accusing him of cannibalism." (Chattanooga *News*, July 11, 1925.) Religious attitudes similar to those prevailing in the South were also to be found in some nonsouthern areas, particularly in rural and small-town communities in the Middle West. (See Robert S. and Helen M. Lynd, *Middletown: A Study in Contemporary American Culture* [New York, 1929], 315–31; and Lewis Atherton, *Main Street on the Middle Border* [Bloomington, Ind., 1954], 258–59.)

tions. Finally, in 1880, a convocation representing Southern Negro Baptist churches, district associations, and state conventions met in Montgomery, Alabama, and founded the Foreign Mission Baptist Convention of the United States. The segregation of Southern Baptists into racially discrete denominations, white and Negro, was now substantially accomplished.[12]

Southern Methodism experienced a similar division. Acting under mandate of the General Conference, the white bishops convened a special Negro conference at Jackson, Tennessee, in December 1870. There the Colored Methodist Episcopal Church in America was organized, two Negro bishops invested, a division of property arranged, and 70,000 Negro communicants transferred from the old church to the new. By 1886 only 527 Negroes remained on the rolls of the parent church.[13] A parallel movement among Southern Presbyterians prevailed in 1898, when the General Assembly approved a plan to transfer its Negro presbyteries to a new Afro-American Presbyterian Church.[14] As early as 1886 the Southern Methodist bishops

[12] Macon, Georgia, *Christian Index*, Feb. 24, Aug. 2, 1866; Shelby County, Alabama, Baptist Association, "Minutes, 1867" (microfilmed by Historical Commission of the Southern Baptist Convention), 145–47, "Minutes, 1868" (microfilmed by Historical Commission of the Southern Baptist Convention), 151; South Carolina State Baptist Convention, *Minutes, 1869* (Columbia, S. C., 1869), 307; Southern Baptist Convention, *Proceedings, 1872* (Baltimore, 1872), 76; Lewis F. Jordan, *Negro Baptist History, U.S.A.* (Nashville, n.d.), 154–71. All Negroes had not yet been removed from the rolls of predominantly white Baptist congregations. As late as 1879, for example, two of twenty-three congregations in the Mississippi Baptist Association (not to be confused with the State Baptist Convention), in southwestern Mississippi, were biracial. Ebenezer Church, in Amite County, included 40 Negroes in its total membership of 146. (Mississippi Baptist Association, *Minutes, 1879* [Natchez, 1879], 34.)

[13] Methodist Episcopal Church, South, General Conference, *Journal, 1870* (Nashville, 1870), 183; *Journal, 1874* (Nashville, 1874), 459, 523; *Journal, 1886* (Nashville, 1886), 18.

[14] Presbyterian Church in the United States, General Assembly, *Minutes, 1898* (Richmond, Va., 1898), 272. All Negro congregations did not transfer to the new church, however. In 1916 the two presbyteries of the Afro-American Presbyterian Church returned to the Presbyterian Church in the United States. The General Assembly merged them with two other all-Negro presbyteries to form the Snedecor Memorial Synod. Most Negro congregations in

conjectured that not "one single colored congregation of any Church in the South [is] served regularly by a white pastor of their own election."[15]

What had begun as a local shuffling into all-white and all-Negro congregations had developed into denominational separation. Negroes spurned the status accorded them in biracial fellowships. The hardened white viewpoint was well articulated by the Methodist bishops, who decried all "sentimental extravagance in the direction of the discolored current of social equality, through the agency of the schoolroom, the congregation, or the Conference; for there is no conceivable result that would compensate for the crime against nature this theory deliberately contemplates."[16] "We must insist," echoed the Mississippi State Baptist Convention of 1891, "that they [Negroes] are distinct, for their good and our's [sic]. To do otherwise is to inflict an evil on them and to raise an insurmountable barrier to success."[17] "Theories of race were as much a part of Southern Baptist thinking as the Virgin Birth or the Second Coming," one student declares.[18]

The outlook in the North was much the same; segregation was the rule and integration the exception throughout the nation. Yet Negroes perceived differences when they crossed the Mason-Dixon line. In the South the color barrier was more precise and the animus aroused by small transgressions more violent and intense. The tide that swept the popular

predominantly white presbyteries were now transferred to this segregated jurisdiction. (Presbyterian Church in the United States, General Assembly, *Minutes, 1916* [Richmond, Va., 1916], 33; *Minutes, 1917* [Richmond, Va., 1917], 30.)

[15] Methodist Episcopal Church, South, General Conference, *Journal, 1886,* 18.

[16] *Ibid.*

[17] Mississippi State Baptist Convention, *Proceedings, 1891* (Jackson, 1891), 22.

[18] Rufus B. Spain, "Attitudes and Reactions of Southern Baptists to Certain Problems of Society, 1865–1900," doctoral dissertation, Vanderbilt University, 1961, 201.

southern churches still worked itself out at the turn of the century. Denominational separation preceded and paralleled movements to compel racial segregation into separate schools, separate railway coaches, separate burying grounds, to exclude Negroes from the ballot, and to deny them vocational opportunities previously afforded.[19]

But central as were ecclesiastical independence and racial segregation to the southern religious ethos, neither shaped the popular churches so much as an all-pervading poverty. In a region lacking adequate resources either for public education or ministerial training, both leadership and response carried the stamp of intellectual backwardness. Episcopalians and Presbyterians normally required a seminary degree for clerical ordination, but other denominations often prescribed nothing more than a call from God. Baptist congregations administering ordination seldom demanded formal schooling. Southern Methodists asked only that candidates be familiar with the Bible, "the ordinary branches of an English education," and John Wesley's sermons "Justification by Faith" and "The Witness of the Spirit"; preachers thus licensed "on trial," however, had to complete a four-year correspondence course before final ordination.[20] Professor F. C. Woodward of Wofford College complained in 1886 that "a man may enter the [Methodist] itinerant ranks without giving to preparation for his great work as much time and pains as would be required to make him a journeyman carpenter! Numbers do . . . who cannot write a complex sentence, or understand it when written. . . ."[21] In 1907 the Nashville *Christian Advocate*

[19] For penetrating studies of these movements, see C. Vann Woodward, *The Strange Career of Jim Crow* (New York, 1957), 13–96, and Rayford W. Logan, *The Negro in American Life and Thought: The Nadir, 1877–1901* (New York, 1954).

[20] *Doctrines and Discipline of the Methodist Episcopal Church, South, 1898* (Nashville, 1898), 287–89.

[21] F. C. Woodward, "Methodism and Ministerial Education," *Southern Methodist Review,* I (Nov. 1886), 212.

lamented that many Methodist clergymen were "totally ignorant" of twentieth-century civilization.[22] As late as 1927 only 4 per cent of the Southern Methodist clergy were seminary graduates, only 11 per cent had college degrees, and approximately 32 per cent had no schooling beyond the elementary level.[23] Nor was there often time in the pastor's crowded routine for extensive independent study. A survey published in 1923 estimated that more than one out of three southern clergymen served four or more churches.[24] Even so, many shared the experience of a Navarro County, Texas, preacher who had to "raise a little cotton" to supplement his clerical earnings. A Baptist leader complained that Baptist rural churches had "won for themselves the pitiful distinction of paying an average wage which is less than a capable field laborer now earns."[25]

Lack of preparation was hardly a handicap in the southern ministry, or so Woodward believed. He grumbled that the Southern Methodist Church "keeps a suspicious eye on its educated young men, but seems to think that ignorance and weakness . . . can be entirely trusted with the charge and oversight of others."[26] The 1906 address of the college of bishops seemed to support this arraignment: "Those who look to the pulpit for spiritual guidance want the authoritative statement of infallible truth, and not the methods of critical research or the varied phases of theological inquiry," the bishops proclaimed.[27] One writer warned in 1887 that "when-

[22] "Who Is to Blame?" in Nashville *Christian Advocate*, Oct. 18, 1907.

[23] "An Episcopal Address: A Better Prepared Ministry," *ibid.*, June 24, 1927. A special Southern Baptist Convention committee on theological education estimated in 1949 that one-third of the Southern Baptist clergy "never went beyond high school." (Southern Baptist Convention, *Book of Reports, 1949* [Nashville, 1949], 310.)

[24] Edmund Brunner, *Church Life in the Rural South* (New York, 1923), 60.

[25] Dallas *Baptist Standard*, July 10, 1902; Victor I. Masters, *Country Church in the South* (Atlanta, 1917), 131.

[26] Woodward, "Methodism and Ministerial Education," 216.

[27] Methodist Episcopal Church, South, General Conference, *Journal, 1906* (Nashville, n.d.,), 40.

ever the day comes that the Methodist Church requires a college course as conditional to admittance to the traveling [preaching] connection, that day will sound the death-knell of the Church." "Send out men whose hearts are hot with love to God," he urged, ". . . and the Holy Ghost will use them to the pulling down of the strongholds of sin and the upbuilding of the kingdom of God and his Christ."[28] The Baptist *Christian Index* approvingly likened the reaction of a congregation to an "earnest" extempore preacher to that between steel and flint—"the sparks fly in all directions."[29]

Despite such sentiment, Southern Methodists and Baptists both sponsored a theological seminary, the Methodist theological school at Vanderbilt University and the Southern Baptist Theological Seminary in Louisville. Southern Presbyterians sponsored four seminaries: Union Theological Seminary (Worsham, Virginia), Columbia (South Carolina) Theological Seminary, Southwestern (Tennessee) Theological Seminary, and the Louisville Theological Seminary. With the exception of Vanderbilt, however, all lacked substantial endowments or other reliable sources of revenue. And all had to contend with a stifling popular distrust of scholarship. Where academic inquiry intruded in the realm of faith, ancient myth was often acclaimed over present truth; this was well illustrated in four celebrated cases.

The first case involved Alexander Winchell, the noted naturalist, who held an appointment as special lecturer at Vanderbilt. Winchell contradicted the account in Genesis of creation in a book entitled *Pre-Adamites*, published in 1878.[30] Seeking to avoid controversy, Vanderbilt officials discreetly asked for his resignation. When he refused, the board of trust promptly abolished his lectureship "to make practical and

[28] W. T. Bolling, " 'Methodism and Ministerial Education,' " *Southern Methodist Review*, II (Mar. 1887), 58–59.

[29] Macon, Georgia, *Christian Index*, Feb. 6, 1890.

[30] Edwin Mims, *History of Vanderbilt University* (Nashville, 1946), 100–102; John James Tiggert IV, *Bishop Holland Nimmons McTyeire, Ecclesiastical and Educational Architect* (Nashville, 1955), 219–23.

needed advances in other departments." Church and university officials did not deny the relevance of Winchell's pronouncements to the board's action, although considerations of economy and efficiency were stressed. The Nashville *Christian Advocate* told how the lectureship "jostled the schedule," was "sort of a fifth wheel," "threw classes and students . . . out of joint."[31]

But talk of reorganization neither misled nor placated the scientist. It was, Winchell insisted, "a dismissal from office on account of heresy," "ecclesiastical proscription for an opinion which must be settled by scientific evidence." He would be "delighted" if the incident stirred wide controversy, which indeed it did.[32] *Popular Science Monthly* scolded the board for "bigotry, intolerance, and proscription" and complained that the "stupid Southern Methodists that control the university, it seems, can learn nothing."[33] In the 1896 edition of his monumental *History of the Warfare of Science with Theology in Christendom*, Andrew D. White portrayed the Vanderbilt episode as one of the "last expiring convulsions of the old theologic theory."[34] Obviously the university's action comported with official Southern Methodist pronouncements. Earlier that year the General Conference pointedly censured those "prominent" scientists who "are bending all the energies of their most exalted genius to the inculcation of theories which are calculated, if not designed, to destroy the credibility of the Holy Scriptures."[35]

Presbyterians reacted similarly toward James Woodrow,

[31] Nashville *Christian Advocate*, July 13, 1878.
[32] Nashville *Daily American*, June 16, 1878.
[33] *Popular Science Monthly*, XIII (Aug. 1878), 492–95.
[34] Andrew D. White, *A History of the Warfare of Science with Theology in Christendom* (2 vols., New York, 1896), I, 85.
[35] Methodist Episcopal Church, South, General Conference, *Journal*, 1878 (Nashville, 1878), 159. Hunter Farish finds that "despite the illiberal utterances occasioned by the Winchell incident, little tendency to heresy hunting was manifested among the Southern Methodists during the remainder of the century. . . ." (Hunter Farish, *The Circuit Rider Dismounts: A Social History of Southern Methodism, 1865–1900* [Richmond, Va., 1938], 297.)

uncle of Woodrow Wilson and professor at the Columbia Theological Seminary. In an address in 1884 Woodrow argued that the theory of evolution could be reconciled with a "not unreasonable interpretation of the Bible" if man's soul were attributed to special creation. He suggested that evolution be construed as "God's PLAN OF CREATION," a "wondrous series of events, caused and controlled by the power and wisdom of the Lord God Almighty. . . ."[36]

A rancorous debate ensued and was carried into the General Assembly of 1886, where Woodrow personally defended his position. But to no avail. By vote of sixty-five to twenty-seven, this highest church tribunal adjudged his statements "repugnant to the Word of God and to our Confession of Faith" and recommended that his professorial appointment be terminated. Seminary trustees then proceeded to dismiss him. Further clarification came from the assembly of 1888: "It is the judgment of this General Assembly that Adam's body was directly fashioned by Almighty God of the dust of the Ground, without any natural animal parentage of any kind."[37]

The Southern Baptist Theological Seminary was embroiled in two such controversies, the first in 1879, when Professor Crawford H. Toy resigned. Toy's resignation followed complaints about his teachings, which purportedly impugned the plenary inspiration of the Scriptures. A committee of the board of trustees scrutinized his written statement of views, interrogated him verbally, and then unanimously recommended that his resignation be accepted. Approval of this recommendation by the full board drew praise from the denominational press. "Under the circumstances," the Macon, Georgia, *Christian Index* declared, "it was manifestly right for

[36] James Woodrow, "Evolution," *Southern Presbyterian Review*, XXXV (July 1884), 341–68.

[37] Presbyterian Church in the United States, General Assembly, *Minutes, 1886* (Columbia, S. C., 1886), 42; *Minutes, 1888* (Richmond, Va., 1888), 399. For a stimulating treatment of the Woodrow episode, see Clement Eaton, "Professor James Woodrow and the Freedom of Teaching in the South," *Journal of Southern History*, XXVIII (Feb. 1962), 3–17.

him to tender his resignation, and equally so for the Board of Trustees to accept." "Our denomination will arm itself against this crusade of vainglorious scholarship," asserted the *Alabama Baptist*: "The fortunes of the kingdom of Jesus Christ are not dependent upon German born vagaries." The Cincinnati *Journal and Messenger* agreed that "no man can maintain good standing in a Baptist Theological Seminary who does not find more of Christ in the prophecies of Isaiah than Prof. Toy does. Baptists greatly prefer the doctrines of Philip and Paul, and Jesus, to those of Prof. Toy." The Richmond *Religious Herald* rejoiced that Toy's successor "is well known and universally loved" and that "there was no risk involved in his appointment."[38]

The reaction of two dissenting trustees was decidedly different. In a strongly worded statement, they chided the board majority for acting precipitously and praised Toy for his "intellectual courage" and "beautiful pattern of loyalty to God's truth." The dissenters also sounded a "sigh and cry for more independence and freedom of thought in the study of the Scriptures" and begged that the seminary not become a mere "manufactory of theological music boxes, all shaped and pitched alike to give forth an unvariable number of invariable tunes." Another Baptist grumbled that Toy had been "guillotined" by a "petrified orthodoxy."[39]

A second altercation two decades later centered around the president of the seminary, William Heth Whitsitt. Like Toy, Whitsitt was an alumnus of the school, and, like Toy, he had joined the faculty after completing advanced study in Germany. His difficulties in the denomination grew out of a historical study of early Baptists, which he pursued for many

---

[38] Richmond *Religious Herald*, May 22, 1879. *The Christian Index* and the *Journal and Messenger* were quoted in the Greenville, South Carolina, *Baptist Courier*, May 29, June 19, 1879; the *Alabama Baptist* was quoted in the Memphis *Baptist*, May 5, 1880.

[39] Greenville, South Carolina, *Baptist Courier*, June 19, 1879, May 6, 1880.

years in the United States and abroad. He first revealed some of his findings in an address at the seminary, in 1880, and subsequently published them in the *Independent* and in a book entitled *A Question in Baptist History*.[40]

Whitsitt prefaced his book with bold assertions that immersion was the only mode of Christian baptism in the New Testament era. "That," he wrote, "is a closed question; it does not admit of being opened among Baptist people." But, having so faithfully affirmed his orthodoxy on this crucial point, he proceeded to recite evidence that the antecedents of American Baptists had erroneously baptized by sprinkling. "Few Anabaptists of any country were immersionists," he concluded, and none of the English Anabaptists immersed before 1641. Moreover, he declared, "within the limits of the uncertainty which is freely acknowledged, the weight appears to incline very clearly towards the view that Roger Williams was sprinkled and not immersed at Providence in 1639." If these conclusions were not to be drawn from the evidence, then "it is useless to prosecute historical investigations of any sort. We may as well close the books, and proceed to evolve our historical conclusions entirely from our own consciousness without any reference to the events that have taken place in the world."[41]

But the evidence left many Baptists unconvinced. Anguished outcries arose from a powerful Landmark faction led by James R. Graves, editor of the Memphis *Baptist*. Landmarkists stressed the congregational structure of the denomination and held aloof from co-operative church enterprises. They emphasized foremost the exclusive correctness of Baptist doctrines

[40] William O. Carver, "William Heth Whitsitt: The Seminary's Martyr," *Review and Expositor*, LI (Oct. 1954), 449–69. See also Isla May Mullins, *Edgar Young Mullins: An Intimate Biography* (Nashville, 1929), 119–25, and A. N. White, *The Life of Rev. Walter Ellis Powers* (Louisville, 1918), 167–71.

[41] William Heth Whitsitt, *A Question in Baptist History* (Louisville, 1896), 5, 48, 127, 164.

and their claim of an unbroken succession of Baptist congregations practicing immersion back to the time of Christ.[42] "Protestant historians frankly admit that Baptist churches are the only religious communities that have stood since the apostles, and as Christian societies, which have preserved pure the doctrine of the gospel through all ages," Graves asserted in 1870. "There is no church but a body of immersed believers who have been immersed by a duly appointed officer of a Scriptural church." Thus the continuity of immersing Baptist congregations was a belief as vital to Landmarkism as the apostolic succession to Catholicism. As early as 1880 Graves charged Whitsitt with heresy and served notice that "we do not want German Rationalism and infidelity taught to our young ministers."[43]

Nevertheless, Whitsitt retained his professorship and was chosen president of the seminary in 1895. Among other apparent aspirants overlooked by the trustees was the Reverend Thomas T. Eaton, pastor of the Louisville Walnut Street Baptist Church, editor of the *Western Recorder*, and chief Landmark spokesman since Graves's death in 1893.[44] Eaton made no attempt to conceal his disgruntlement. "We in America are fast drifting toward a state of things which has long existed in Germany, where the freedom of theological professors is complete," he complained. "A man who is an atheist may be a professor of theology in Germany, and it is all right. We have not reached that point in this country, but we are drifting in that direction." He published an article declaring that "whoever attempts to prove that the church system of the New Testament has ever been extinct . . . is neither a good Baptist nor a safe logician, however skilled in history." One contributor to the *Western Recorder* charged

[42] James R. Graves, *Old Landmarkism: What Is It?* (Texarkana, Tex., 1928), 140–41, 228.

[43] Memphis *Baptist*, Jan. 8, 1870, May 12, 1880.

[44] Eaton and Whitsitt were among three prospects formally considered by the board. (Carver, "William Heth Whitsitt," 463.)

that anyone denying the historical continuity of Baptist churches practicing immersion "is an infidel."[45]

Strong words were accompanied by equally strong deeds. In 1897 the Kentucky State Baptist Association formally demanded Whitsitt's resignation, and the following year voted to withhold support from the school as long as he continued in office. At least five other state organizations and numerous district associations took similar action. Reacting to the protests, seminary trustees invited the harassed president to elucidate his historical findings before them in 1897. "I can do no otherwise than to reaffirm my position," he told the board. "But if in the future it should ever be made to appear that I have erred in my conclusions I would promptly and cheerfully say so. I am a searcher after truth. . . ." The board voted to retain him in office, declaring itself unqualified to "sit in judgment on questions in Baptist history." Again, in 1898, Whitsitt was re-elected, but this time the board equivocated by setting up a special committee to exercise continuous surveillance over the school.[46]

It had become apparent, however, that Whitsitt's attackers would settle for nothing short of unconditional surrender; indeed, it now seemed clear that they would strive to destroy the seminary if he continued as its head. Nor could their power in the Southern Baptist Convention be ignored. In 1898 the convention refused to make nominations to fill vacancies on the board of trustees, and designated instead a committee to study the advisability "of changing the present relation of the Convention to the Seminary." The Reverend B. H. Carroll of Waco, Texas (later president of the Southwestern Baptist Theological Seminary), announced he would sponsor a move at the next convention to terminate "the slight

[45] Louisville *Western Recorder*, June 16, 28, 1898.

[46] *Ibid.*, June 23, July 7, 1898; Memphis *Baptist and Reflector*, May 12, 1897, May 26, June 30, 1898; T. A. Patterson, "The Theology of J. R. Graves and Its Influence on Southern Baptist Life," doctoral dissertation, Southwestern Baptist Theological Seminary, 1944, 270–76.

and remote bond of connection between this body and the Seminary."[47]

Stung by the ferocity of the attack, Whitsitt reluctantly decided to yield. On July 13, 1898, he submitted his resignation, effective at the close of the 1898–1899 session. "We have learned with much satisfaction of the resignation of Dr. Whitsitt," a resolution of the Mississippi State Baptist Convention declared. "Accepting his resignation as a fact in good faith, we deem this an opportune time to reaffirm our loyalty to the Seminary and pledge to it our most hearty support." A Texas Baptist rejoiced that "sentiment and help will again flow as a current toward the Seminary." Eaton suggested "it might be well that the trustees should meet immediately and accept his resignation." Although the trustees ignored Eaton's advice, they did accept the resignation at their regular meeting the following spring. Thus was harmony restored between the seminary, the Southern Baptist Convention, and state and district Baptist associations. The convention committee designated to consider "changing the present relation of the Convention to the Seminary" made no recommendation; Carroll announced he no longer favored withdrawing Baptist sponsorship from the school.[48]

Of course faculty removals for doctrinal unorthodoxy were not a peculiarly southern eccentricity. But the actions against Winchell, Woodrow, Toy, and Whitsitt—involving as they did the highest authority in all three major white denominations—evidenced a general and concerted reluctance to reexamine traditional precepts. It was the degree of consensus on such issues that distinguished the South. Little-educated clergymen nurtured and perpetuated the consensus, as did

[47] Southern Baptist Convention, *Annual, 1898* (Atlanta, n.d.), 23, 34; *Dr. B. H. Carroll, The Colossus of Baptist History*, ed. J. W. Crowder (Fort Worth, 1946), 132.

[48] Memphis *Baptist and Reflector*, July 21, Sept. 8, 1898; Louisville *Western Recorder*, July 21, 1898; Southern Baptist Convention, *Annual, 1899* (Atlanta, n.d.), 18.

ecclesiastical structures wherein the laity exercised a powerful voice. Among both clergy and rank and file there was an awesome reverence for the Bible, literally construed, and a hypersensitivity toward any subversion of hallowed beliefs.[49]

If little attention was given to newer theological interpretations, even less was given to the application of Christian teachings to the social milieu. A Baptist historian finds that editors of Baptist journals in the southeastern states failed during this era "to perceive any relation between Christian morality and economic justice" and "showed little compassion toward industrial employees."[50] This was surely true of an analysis published in the Georgia Baptist *Christian Index*, in 1900:

The majority of the poor, "the submerged tenth," the begrimed masses who swarm in the slums and wretched tenement houses of our large cities, some of whom are also found in the smaller towns and even in the country, are dissipated, vicious, wicked and immoral. Many reformers of the day teach that, if you improve their surroundings and educate them, you can lift them up. Far be it from me to discourage any efforts along this line of work; but what these people need is to be made over again. There is but one power in the world that can do this, and that is the gospel of the Son of God.[51]

Earlier the *Index* had bitterly assailed the Pullman strikers. The remedy it advocated was "the bayonet and the bullet, promptly and fearlessly applied. Gentleness in dealing with such outlaws is simply cruel injustice to law abiding, peaceable

---

[49] "It seems an inescapable inference," one writer declares, "that in the sphere of religion the Southerner has always been hostile to the spirit of inquiry." (R. M. Weaver, "The Older Religiousness in the South," *Sewanee Review*, LI [Apr.–June 1943], 248.)

[50] Carl D. English, "The Ethical Emphases of the Editors of Baptist Journals Published in the Southeastern Region of the United States, 1865–1915," doctoral dissertation, Southern Baptist Theological Seminary, 1948, 248, 285.

[51] T. M. Galphin, "Christianity and Temporal Prosperity," in Macon, Georgia, *Christian Index*, Aug. 30, 1900.

citizens."[52] But only in matters relating to pious conduct—blasphemy, gambling, drinking, divorce, sabbath observance, and the like—did southern churchmen strive often to influence public policy before 1900.[53]

Essentially, religious thought in the South had changed little since the era of frontier revivalism. An almost single-minded emphasis on individual regeneration remained. Sermons abounded in expositions on salvation, the joys of heaven, and the horrors of hell; often they were a recital of the clergyman's "personal emotional experience and nothing else."[54] A Baptist leader complained that "with gratifying but all-too-few exceptions, our country preachers confine themselves largely to evangelistic sermons."[55] In an address before the Southern Baptist Convention in 1899 George W. Truett, pastor of the Dallas First Baptist Church and a renowned pulpit orator, belittled ministers who expounded "philosophy, or science, or culture, or worldly wisdom." "Sooner far," he declared, "let us commend to the lips of a famished child a painted glass, filled with painted water . . . or to a heart-broken mother a poem on the north pole. . . ." He ridiculed "screaming voices which propose to adjust discordant elements in both church and state," the "great itch abroad in the land demanding 'reform,'" and insisted that the message of the church must be the simple message of personal redemption through Jesus Christ.[56] Similarly, in 1902, the Southern Methodist bishops eulogized early leaders of their church, noting that they had not been "hindered in their work by a seeming obligation to instruct the people in philosophy and science and all sociological problems as platform lecturers. . . ."[57]

[52] Quoted in Spain, "Attitudes and Reactions of Southern Baptists," 233.
[53] Ibid., 317, 363; Farish, Circuit Rider Dismounts, 369.
[54] Brunner, Church Life in the Rural South, 74.
[55] Masters, Country Church, 99.
[56] The American Baptist Pulpit at the Beginning of the Twentieth Century, ed. Henry T. Louthan (Williamsburg, Va., 1903), 254–73.
[57] Methodist Episcopal Church, South, General Conference, Journal, 1902 (Nashville, n.d.), 22.

Popular hymns warned of the uncertainty of human existence. A hymn in the official Southern Methodist *Hymnal* cautioned that

> Death rides on every passing breeze,
>   And lurks in every flower;
> Each season has its own disease,
>   Its peril every hour![58]

A selection in the Southern Baptist *Hymn and Praise Book* warned of

> That day of wrath, that dreadful day,
>   When heav'n and earth shall pass away!
> What pow'r shall be the sinner's stay?
>   How shall we meet that dreadful day?[59]

A North Carolina minister's sermon on "Heavenly Recognition" conjectured that earthly friendships would be renewed after death and that "pastors will meet their dear flocks there and rejoice with them." The editor of the Methodist Raleigh *Christian Advocate* visualized the "hosts of the redeemed gathering about the great White Throne. . . . They are clothed in garments of white, with crowns of rejoicing upon their brows, and golden harps suspended on their arms, and palms of victory in their hands." Another North Carolina clergyman wrote that "it is sad to say farewell to those who are dying; but how sweet to think of greeting [them] on the eternal shore of rest, sweet rest."[60]

Emotional responses attested the soul-stirring potency of such themes. In 1900 the Reverend Franklin H. Kerfoot, one-time professor at the Southern Baptist Theological Seminary and later corresponding secretary of the Southern Baptist Home Mission Board, delivered a sermon before the Texas

[58] *Hymn and Tune Book of the Methodist Episcopal Church, South* (Nashville, 1894), 297.

[59] *Baptist Hymn and Praise Book* (Nashville, 1904), Hymn No. 538.

[60] *North Carolina Sermons*, ed. Levi Branson (3 vols., Raleigh, 1893), III, 33, 182, 309.

State Baptist Convention. Kerfoot dwelt on the inevitability of human suffering: "tribulations, and persecutions, and famine, and nakedness, and sword. . . ." The only hope was that "God will not forsake us in death. . . . Nothing shall separate us from His love then." Kerfoot's passionate affirmation of this hope, following his dreary portrayal of hopelessness, evoked a turbulent demonstration. A correspondent of the Raleigh *Biblical Recorder* described the scene:

The congregation rose and sang "How Firm a Foundation," while men shouted, wept, and embraced, and struggled to express the inexpressible joy within them. Think of an audience of twenty-five hundred people rushing and surging to shake hands and embrace, climbing over chairs, waving hands and handkerchiefs. It was wonderful—wonderful![61]

Although camp meetings had been generally supplanted by more decorous indoor services, most southern congregations still sponsored special evangelistic campaigns each year.[62] The revival season in July and August, after the crops were laid by, was a major focus and outlet. Southern Baptists "often seem . . . to regard evangelism as the be-all and end-all of religion," one critic complained.[63] It was an indictment applicable also to most other Protestants. C. Vann Woodward tells of two North Carolina counties where an aggregate of 211 revivals was conducted in one year during this era![64] Religious newspapers devoted lengthy columns to revivals; a few reports published in 1900 are illustrative. A South Carolina dispatch related that the "village of McClellanville has just passed through one of the happiest revivals that has ever been con-

[61] Louthan, *American Baptist Pulpit*, 733–51.

[62] Charles A. Johnson, *The Frontier Camp Meeting: Religion's Harvest Time* (Dallas, 1955), is an able treatment. Revivalism in this century is surveyed in William G. McLoughlin, Jr., *Modern Revivalism: Charles Grandison Finney to Billy Graham* (New York, 1959).

[63] Dixon, "Southern Baptists through Northern Eyes."

[64] C. Vann Woodward, *Origins of the New South, 1877–1913* (Baton Rouge, 1951), 452.

ducted in that section of the coast country." The pastor of the Dalton, Georgia, Methodist Church announced that "for three weeks, during a downpour of rain day and night, the greatest revival Dalton ever had has been going on" and that "practically the whole city [is] revived." A participant in an East Macon, Georgia, revival wrote that "I never saw such a meeting. It looked as if the entire community had professed conversion."[65] The Lexington, Mississippi, Baptist Church likened its revival to "a cluster of rich grapes! We crushed them and drank the sacred wine and by faith inhaled the fragrant spices of the 'empty tomb.'" At Union Baptist Church, in Tippah County, Mississippi, the service that was to conclude a revival ended "with a good old-time handshaking while the membership sang, with feeling, 'Amazing Grace,' with chorus, 'We'll all sing Hallelujah.' The interest was so marked . . . that it was thought best to continue the meeting. . . ." A report from the Hermansville, Mississippi, Baptist Church described their revival as a "spiritual earthquake."[66] Luxora, Arkansas, Methodists felt they were "on high ground, having just closed one of the most successful meetings ever held in the county"; in that same state a report from the little town of Nashville declared that "our whole community was moved and touched" by a series of evangelistic services. From Texas came an account of a Methodist revival on the Glenwood Charge, near Forth Worth, where "there was evident the 'old-time power,' as Christians were made happy and shouted."[67] Participants also "shouted as of old, and gave unmistakable evidence of religious joy" during a "most glorious" revival at Oak Grove Baptist Church, in Navarro County, Texas;[68] Nacona, Texas, Methodists told of being swept by a "spiritual wave."[69]

[65] Nashville *Christian Advocate*, June 28, Aug. 9, Nov. 1, 1900.
[66] Jackson *Baptist Record*, July 26, Aug. 11, 16, 1900.
[67] Nashville *Christian Advocate*, July 19, Aug. 16, Oct. 18, 1900.
[68] Dallas *Baptist Standard*, July 10, 1900.
[69] Nashville *Christian Advocate*, Mar. 22, 1900.

But few revivals of the year produced such evidences of success as that of the Scottsville, Kentucky, Methodist Church. A published account noted that "we used old-time methods; had the mourners bench, and preached and prayed until conviction seized the sinner and invited him to come." Results seemed to vindicate this procedure. More than ninety professed conversion, and an unestimated number were "reclaimed." Among the converts were the county attorney, city attorney, city marshal, district clerk, jailer, "and other representative men of the city."[70]

Where religious passions surged to a high tide, revivals were often protracted. In 1900 Methodist revivals at Tracy City, Tennessee, and Scottsville, Kentucky, lasted three weeks, while Russellville, Arkansas, Methodists were "blessed with a great meeting, which continued more than three weeks." Another meeting at Dalton, Georgia, continued three weeks and then was extended for "another week at least." The Knoxville Highland Avenue Methodist Church entered its sixth week of revival services in February 1900 "with added enthusiasm and zeal." In July 1904 the pastor of the Cherokee Avenue Baptist Church, at Gaffney, South Carolina, reported "almost a continous [sic] revival for the past two months." That same year the Waco, Texas, First Baptist Church sponsored revival services twice a day for a period of almost two months. But the New Orleans *Christian Advocate* complained in 1900 that "most meetings have closed too soon to get great ingatherings."[71]

Normally revivals were evaluated according to number of conversions, although other results were not overlooked. During one east Tennessee revival, "many old neighborhood feuds" were said to have been settled. A Baptist revivalist in a turbulent area of southeastern Mississippi, "where they kill

[70] *Ibid.*, Mar. 8, 1900.
[71] *Ibid.*, Feb. 15, Mar. 8, June 28, July 19, Aug. 30, 1900; Greenville, South Carolina, *Baptist Courier*, July 21, 1904; Powhatan W. James, *George W. Truett, A Biography* (Nashville, 1953), 74–76.

men and threaten preachers" and where the meeting house "had the sign of buckshot about the door that stole the life of a man," hoped he had been "at least some help" in promoting tranquillity. A revival report from Fairmont, South Carolina, told of only one addition to the church, but rejoiced that "the church was strengthened spiritually." Occasionally contributions to religious causes were stimulated. During one meeting, $508 was collected for a religious education fund; during another, a $650 parsonage debt was paid; and, at Jackson, Tennessee, a church board increased the Methodist minister's salary during a revival.[72]

Not all southerners regarded revivalism as an unmixed blessing. A Cameron, Texas, Baptist boasted that his congregation's revival "was not of the evangelistic order, and it is hoped that our religion will not be of a spasmodic kind, manifesting itself principally during revivals and conspicuous by its absence at other times." A South Carolina Baptist opined that "we are taught that the gospel should be preached that sinners might be converted, and not that excitement shall be created to strengthen the church numerically." The Nashville *Christian Advocate* cautioned that excitement should not be "churned up by artificial stimulants, and looked upon as an end in itself." "Morbid and unnatural excitement of the human emotions disturbs the balance of the faculties, enfeebles the will, and leads on to gross immorality," the *Advocate* warned. The Southern Methodist bishops noted with displeasure in 1894 that "many communities are restless unless they have weeks of evangelistic meetings yearly. . . ." There were frequent complaints about the substitution of "jerky, ditty-like" songs for the more restrained selections of the official hymnals.[73]

[72] Nashville *Christian Advocate*, Feb. 15, May 24, June 28, 1900; Jackson *Baptist Record*, July 26, 1900; Greenville, South Carolina, *Baptist Courier*, Sept. 4, 1904.
[73] Dallas *Baptist Standard*, June 26, 1902; Greenville, South Carolina, *Baptist Courier*, Sept. 8, 1904; Nashville *Christian Advocate*, May 31, June

But complaints and warnings did little to curb revival enthusiasm. Revivals flourished, most of all, because they fulfilled vital needs in southern society. They brought hope to many who knew little of hope and release to many who knew little of release. The revival preacher communicated his zest and zeal to others. With an intensity, a cadence, an intonation peculiar to his craft, resorting often to violent gestures, he played on themes of pain and sorrow, passion and pathos, love and redemption. Thus were the lost shepherded into the fold and the hope of believers rekindled. Significantly, also, revivals afforded a welcome respite from rural isolation. Visiting, the renewal of old acquaintances, and courting among the young people were more than incidental accompaniments of the revival season.

And so the South remained a land of piety and tradition. "There is no part of the world in which ministers of the Gospel are more respected than in the Southern states," a distinguished Methodist editor declared.[74] The Reverend H. C. Morrison of Asbury College doubted whether there was "another territory of like area beneath the sun, where there is a stronger, better faith in the Bible, where the Sabbath is better observed, where a larger per cent. of the people attend church, and where virtue in womanhood and honesty in manhood are more common and command a better premium."[75] A preoccupation with individual repentance, a dogged insistence on Biblical inerrancy, a tendency toward overt expression of intense religious emotions: these legacies of frontier revivalism still held a primacy. Of this most southerners were proud.

28, Sept. 6, 1900; Methodist Episcopal Church, South, General Conference, *Journal, 1894* (Nashville, n.d.), 24–25.

[74] Nashville *Christian Advocate*, Oct. 17, 1885, quoted in Farish, *Circuit Rider Dismounts*, 105.

[75] Atlanta *Southern Presbyterian*, Aug. 10, 1905.

2

EDUCATION AND SOCIAL CONCERN, 1900-1917

*T*he commitment to evangelism and spiritual nurture was never quite so total as was often asserted. Churchmen had risen in defense of slavery before the Civil War. When war came they blessed the military efforts of the Confederacy. In the postwar years they championed home rule and racial segregation. Preachers could not ignore the world about them even if they strove to do so. Ecclesiastical estrangement from northern Protestantism made the southern denominations peculiarly regional in tone and temper. They interacted with indigenous elements in their society and were molded by many of the forces that molded other institutions. When the churches intruded in temporal spheres, it was as if the South belonged to them as much as they belonged to the South.

Education had always been a major ecclesiastical concern,

though concern was usually unmatched by resources. From 1874 to 1902 the number of colleges sponsored by the Southern Methodist Church declined from fifty to eighteen.[1] Complaining that the "disease of starting Baptist Colleges has been sporadic, endemic, and epidemic," a committee of the Southern Baptist Convention belittled a group which was "cutting poles" for a new college in 1907.[2] This was in a state where sixteen Baptist colleges had been founded during the preceding half century, only nine of which survived. Yet such attritions signified no over-all slackening of effort. Consolidations and reclassifications as secondary schools accounted for the demise of many so-called "colleges." At the turn of the century 13,859 of 26,237 students attending southern universities, colleges, and schools of technology were enrolled in church-related institutions.[3]

The central function of denominational schools was the training of preachers. But a quickening interest in popular education was evident among churchmen in the post-Civil War era. This was in part a reaction to public schools. "As it is not the business of the state to teach religion," grumbled the Georgia Baptist *Christian Index* in 1890, "it therefore ought not to make education a part of its business."[4] Nineteen years earlier the Southern Presbyterian General Assembly had proclaimed that education was "too dear, too vital to us as a Church, to be remitted to the State, to other communions, or to any irresponsible body of educators. . . ."[5] The Southern Methodist bishops avowed in 1874 "that we regard the edu-

---

[1] Methodist Episcopal Church, South, General Conference, *Journal*, 1874, 582; *Journal*, 1902, 34–35.

[2] Southern Baptist Convention, *Annual*, 1907 (Nashville, n.d.), 28.

[3] US Department of Interior, Bureau of Education, *Report of the Commissioner of Education*, 1899–1900 (2 vols., Washington, D. C., 1901), II, 1878–79, 1904–23, 1944–53. Enrollment statistics are for Kentucky, Oklahoma, and the eleven states of the former Confederacy.

[4] Macon, Georgia, *Christian Index*, July 17, 1890.

[5] Presbyterian Church in the United States, General Assembly, *Minutes*, 1871 (Columbia, S. C., 1871), 17.

cation of the young as one of the leading functions of the Church, and that she cannot abdicate in favor of the State without infidelity to her trust and irreparable damage to society"; free tuition at state schools could not compensate "for the risk of diverting a young heart and life from the noblest end of its being!"[6] The *Christian Index* argued that "the tendency of the [public school] system is to communism, to the denial of individual rights in property. When the state puts its hand into the pocket of one of its citizens, and takes out his money to pay the tuition of another man's child, it has taken a long step towards the destruction of all distinctions between 'mine and thine.' "[7]

Southern Methodists laid ambitious plans to sponsor mass education. The 1874 General Conference recommended a denominational boarding school for "every District in our work," a proposal which the bishops endorsed as the "only antidote to that godless feature in the public school which ignores the Holy Scriptures in the training of youth."[8] A contributor to the Southern Methodist *Quarterly Review* urged that public education be curtailed to accommodate such efforts; let the states restrict themselves to elementary schools and universities, he demanded, leaving academies and colleges to the churches, "for the reason that these latter have so much to do in the formation of moral character."[9] On the other hand, the *Christian Index* wanted each local congregation to "have its own school, taught by teachers who are well grounded in its own faith and practice."[10]

---

[6] Methodist Episcopal Church, South, General Conference, *Journal*, 1874, 387; *Journal*, 1886, 23.

[7] Macon, Georgia, *Christian Index*, July 17, 1890. Rufus B. Spain believes that by 1890 a majority of Southern Baptists supported the principle of public education. (Spain, "Attitudes and Reactions of Southern Baptists," 70.)

[8] Methodist Episcopal Church, South, General Conference, *Journal*, 1874, 507; *Journal*, 1878, 36.

[9] F. M. Edwards, "Systems of Education," *Quarterly Review of the Methodist Episcopal Church, South*, VI (Oct. 1884), 667–83.

[10] Macon, Georgia, *Christian Index*, Feb. 27, 1890.

The Methodist bishops rendered a succession of optimistic reports on the progress of their church's secondary schools. Calling for further expansions, they hailed the success of the program as a "gratifying fact" in 1882. Four years later they rejoiced that "no part of our educational system promises a better return." In 1890 they looked forward to the time when attendance in a denominational school "will become the common right of all the children of the Church. . . ." But zeal and hope obscured meager accomplishments. Methodist secondary schools were obviously on the wane by the 1890's, and the bishops conceded in 1902 that "we have possibly lost more of these schools than we have saved." The General Conference responded with a resolution "not so much [to] seek to establish new secondary schools as properly to care for such as have proved themselves worthy." Equally significant was the 1902 conference's pledge of "active cooperation" in the "improvement of the [public] common schools in the rural districts of the South. . . ."[11] The authoritative Nashville *Christian Advocate* spoke more emphatically several years later. "All schools, whether public or private, that will ensure the partial education at least of every child should be encouraged," the *Advocate* declared. "The battle against ignorance is on, and the Church is ready to join the State in any campaign that will result in the wiping out of the disgrace of illiteracy. . . ."[12]

Methodist efforts in southern education probably surpassed those of any other group or agency before the turn of the century. Scores of Methodist colleges and secondary schools

[11] Methodist Episcopal Church, South, General Conference, *Journal*, 1882, 23; *Journal*, 1886, 24; *Journal*, 1890 (Nashville, 1890), 39; *Journal*, 1902, 33, 228.

[12] Nashville *Christian Advocate*, Sept. 27, 1907. Hunter Farish discusses the Methodist secondary schools in his *Circuit Rider Dismounts*, 242–49. He finds a growing tolerance toward public education among Methodist leaders in the 1880's. During that decade, some Southern Methodist journals supported the Blair bill, which would have allocated federal funds for public education.

functioned at a time when state education was little more than a hope for the future. In founding Vanderbilt University, Methodists gave the postwar South its first institution with an academic standing somewhat equivalent to that of better northern universities. Moreover, Methodists made enormous contributions in helping to inaugurate standards of accreditation. A Southern Methodist Commission of Education was organized in the 1890's to grade and evaluate church institutions. At about the same time, Vanderbilt officials took the lead in organizing a regional accrediting agency for both secular and church schools, the Association of Colleges and Preparatory Schools for the Southern States. By the turn of the century, after an earlier period of hostility, most Methodist leaders championed public elementary and secondary schools.[13]

Baptist and Presbyterian attitudes closely paralleled those of the Methodists. "God believes in education," the Southern Baptist Convention declared in 1913.[14] But endorsements of public schools were often coupled with demands that they operate under a religious influence. In 1917 the Southern Baptist Education Commission hoped for the day "when only God-fearing men and women may teach in our state schools, from the common school to the university. . . ."[15] "What we want, therefore, are converted men and women in charge of our schools," the Chickasahay (Mississippi) Baptist Association resolved in 1900; "and not to do what one can to insure this, is to criminally jeopardise the best interests of the young."[16] "Christianize our School Boards and our army of teachers," urged the New Orleans *Southwestern Presbyterian,* "and the problem would be solved without the Church, as such, em-

---

[13] Farish, *Circuit Rider Dismounts,* 245, 254, 278. See also Woodward, *Origins of the New South,* 439.

[14] Southern Baptist Convention, *Annual, 1913* (Nashville, n.d.), 60.

[15] Southern Baptist Convention, *Annual, 1917* (Nashville, n.d.), 67–68.

[16] Chickasahay Baptist Association, *Minutes, 1900* (Meridian, Miss., n.d.), 14.

barking in secular education."[17] "The Christian citizens of a
country owe it to themselves, their children, the State and
their Lord," declared the Southern Presbyterian General Assembly in 1904, "to be faithful in protecting public schools
from the evils of influences unfriendly to Christianity. . . ."
The 1906 assembly approved two specific objectives: to secure
"the appointment of moral and Christian teachers" and to
"place the Bible in all schools, along with some simple forms
of worship every day, wherever it is practicable."[18] Such peti-
tions were not ignored. Chancellor James H. Kirkland of Vanderbilt University affirmed in 1910 that throughout the region
"no unfriendly attitude has been shown to religion either in
the lower schools or in the State universities. The Bible is
generally read in the public schools, and often school is opened
with a song and prayer."[19] The Nashville *Christian Advocate*
rejoiced that "the South is the stronghold of religious education. In no other section of our country are there proportion-
ately so many Church schools or so general a religious influence pervading the public schools."[20]

Denominational sponsorship of higher education continued
on a major scale. Although one Southern Presbyterian committee reported in 1906 that "our Church colleges for young
men were never more prosperous," another called for vast
expansions in Presbyterian higher education to "hold the
young people of the South true to genuine spiritual religion."
The latter committee emphasized that Southern Baptists and
Methodists had "steadily and zealously emphasized this

[17] New Orleans *Southwestern Presbyterian*, July 26, 1900.
[18] Presbyterian Church in the United States, General Assembly, *Minutes,
1904* (Richmond, Va., 1904), 38; *Minutes, 1906* (Richmond, 1906), 115.
A survey in 1923 revealed that daily Bible reading in public schools was required by law in Alabama, Tennessee, Georgia, and in three northern states
(New Jersey, Massachusetts, and Pennsylvania); the practice was legally
permissible in thirty-two other states. (US Department of Interior, Bureau
of Education, *Bulletin, 1923*, No. 15.)
[19] James H. Kirkland, "Progress in Religious and Moral Education," in
Nashville *Christian Advocate*, Mar. 25, 1910.
[20] Nashville *Christian Advocate*, Feb. 11, 1910.

branch of church work . . . till they have become relatively stronger in our section than anywhere else in the world."[21] The 1913 Southern Baptist Convention called for "at least one absolutely first-rate [Baptist] college in every state within the bounds of this Convention." The Bayou Macon (Louisiana) Baptist Association boasted in 1922 that "American Baptists have invested a larger amount of money in their schools than any other denomination in the United States."[22] Few church leaders doubted that the cause was worth the effort. A Southern Presbyterian committee warned that professors in state colleges often "arraign Christianity at the bar of rationalistic philosophy and an agnostic science, and pass adverse sentence on all we count dear."[23] One vital feature of church-controlled education was portrayed in published accounts of a revival at Methodist Emory and Henry College. "Professors, young ministers, and laymen alike aided the pastor by zealous personal work, and were loath to give up until the last student had professed a saving faith in Christ"; at the close of the meeting "there were left only seven who had not enlisted in the service of the Master."[24] "Alas!" resolved the Southern Baptist Convention in 1913 "for that [Baptist] college which passes a single session and leaves all its unconverted students still unconverted. And, alas, for that college whose students return home at the close of the session to be less useful to their churches than they were before they left."[25]

Denominational education suffered a frustrating setback in 1914, when the Southern Methodist Church broke its ties with Vanderbilt University. Founded in 1873 and endowed by the eccentric Commodore and his family, Vanderbilt at first operated under the auspices of several annual conferences.

[21] Presbyterian Church in the United States, General Assembly, *Minutes*, 1906, 113, 126–27.
[22] Southern Baptist Convention, *Annual, 1913*, 61; Bayou Macon Baptist Association, *Minutes*, 1922 (n.p., n.d.), 12.
[23] Presbyterian Church in the United States, *Minutes*, 1906, 115.
[24] Nashville *Christian Advocate*, Apr. 12, May 3, 1900.
[25] Southern Baptist Convention, *Annual, 1913*, 61.

Later it passed under the unique sponsorship of the General Conference. The bishops proudly acclaimed it in 1902 as "the head of our education system." In 1910 the chairman of the General Conference Committee on Education acknowledged the university as "by far the most potent influence in the South outside the Church."[26]

Relations between the church and the university deteriorated after 1905, when the board of trust repealed one of its bylaws which had designated all Southern Methodist bishops *ex officio* trustees. Now only five senior bishops could sit with the board. The board's action was challenged, and the precise legal authority of the church over the school brought into discussion. An attempt by the 1910 General Conference to fill vacancies on the board without consulting the incumbents, and efforts by the bishops to exercise a veto right over board decisions, were hotly resisted. In the prolonged litigation which followed, legal arguments were accompanied by unusually bitter exchanges outside court. The editor of the Nashville *Christian Advocate* grumbled that the faculty and a majority of the trustees believed that "the further away the Church keeps from its institutions the better the interests of the institutions will be subserved [sic]," and that the university's course reflected a "defiant, hitherto victorious advance of secularized education." "You cannot send a boy to Vanderbilt University to be educated without having his mind poisoned against the Methodist Church," a delegate to the General Conference in 1914 complained.[27]

Rejoinders came from the university community. Chancellor Kirkland asserted that "from the beginning of Vanderbilt

[26] Methodist Episcopal Church, South, General Conference, *Journal, 1902*, 35; *Daily Christian Advocate, 1910* (Asheville, 1910), 83. An excellent account of the break between Vanderbilt and the Southern Methodist Church appears in Mims, *History of Vanderbilt University*, 291–318. See also Isaac Patton Martin, *Elijah Embree Hoss* (Nashville, 1942), 282–306.

[27] Nashville *Christian Advocate*, July 19, 1914; Methodist Episcopal Church, South, General Conference, *Daily Christian Advocate, 1914* (Oklahoma City, 1914), 89, 92.

history the College of Bishops has occupied an unenviable position toward this enterprise." The bishops had "withheld their cooperation and support" in founding the university, the Chancellor averred, had opposed the creation of a theological school, and had displayed often "an attitude of antagonism."[28] Charges and countercharges waxed hotter after Andrew Carnegie announced his tentative allocation of $1,000,000 to the university medical school. The bulk of the grant was contingent on a court ruling favorable to the board of trust since Carnegie believed it unwise "for any sect to control educational institutions such as universities." When the board welcomed the offer along with a $200,000 advance payment, the bishops proceeded to "veto said action and every part thereof and declare the same null and void."[29] In apparent reference to Kirkland, the Nashville *Christian Advocate* quoted from Matthew 4:8–9. "Again, the devil taketh him up into an exceeding high mountain, and showeth him all the kingdoms of the world, and the glory of them; and saith unto him, All these things will I give thee, if thou wilt fall down and worship me."[30]

On March 21, 1914, the Tennessee Supreme Court handed down its final ruling. The court held that the charter under which the university operated did not assign to the bishops a veto right; nor did it permit the General Conference to elect trustees other than candidates nominated by the incumbents. In case of a deadlock with the church, the board could perpetuate itself. Vanderbilt students celebrated the ruling with a bonfire; a group also moved through downtown Nashville performing what was mockingly acclaimed as the "Bishop's Squirm."[31]

In angry disgruntlement, the General Conference now terminated its relationship with Vanderbilt and channeled its

[28] Nashville *Christian Advocate,* July 4, 1913.
[29] *Ibid.,* June 27, 1913.
[30] *Ibid.,* July 11, 1913.
[31] *Ibid.,* Apr. 10, 1914.

support to new theological schools at Emory University and Southern Methodist University. The presiding elders and the Board of Education of the North Mississippi Annual Conference no doubt voiced a widespread apprehension when they demanded that the new seminaries be "free from every taint of heresy" and that "the atmosphere enveloping these institutions should by every token be kept thoroughly spiritual and evangelical." Bishop J. C. Kilgo gave assurance that Emory's theological faculty was "as sound in faith as they are superior in scholarly attainments" and that they would "not confuse the minds of students with useless doubts."[32]

A resolution adopted by the Southern Baptist Convention in 1913 shows that apprehensions of this nature were not confined to Methodist ranks. The convention demanded that "the denomination ought to have such control of its colleges as will make speedy correction possible when the college begins to verge from the doctrine or spirit of the New Testament." But there seemed little evidence that Baptist institutions veered far from orthodox paths. Teachers in Baptist schools were "earnestly seeking to safeguard their students against error," the convention was advised in 1923. "Where books have been found unsatisfactory and yet are the best obtainable, the professors have been careful to supplement the text books with lectures."[33]

Church control also entailed broad social ramifications, or so Asa G. Candler believed. In contributing $1,000,000 to Emory University after the Vanderbilt defection, this Coca-Cola magnate and brother of Bishop Warren A. Candler proclaimed that "what our country needs is not more secular education, but more of the education that is fundamentally and intentionally religious." He was convinced that the South's "evangelical and brotherly type of Christianity," which he

[32] *Ibid.*, Aug. 28, Oct. 9, 1914.
[33] Southern Baptist Convention, *Annual, 1913*, 61; *Annual, 1923* (Nashville, n.d.), 31.

expected Emory to perpetuate, made for "a wholesome conservatism politically and socially, and for a blessed civilization crowned with piety and peace."[34]

Yet the southern churches were less wholesomely conservative than Candler might have wished. Nor were schools and pulpits their only means of influence and inculcation. Departing from a policy previously well defined, they resorted increasingly to political agitation in the two decades before World War I. "Our Church is strictly a religious and in no wise a political body," the Southern Methodist bishops had proclaimed as late as 1894. "The more closely we keep ourselves to the one work of testifying to all men repentance toward God and faith toward our Lord Jesus Christ, the better shall we promote the highest good of our country and race."[35] In 1888 the president of the Southern Baptist Convention rejected an attempt to commit the convention on the politically charged issue of legal prohibition. He ruled two prohibition resolutions irrelevant to the convention's specified functions of "eliciting, combining and directing the energies of the whole denomination in one sacred effort for the propagation of the gospel. . . ."[36]

Of course the churches had always extolled righteous conduct. The Southern Presbyterian General Assembly ruled in 1893, for example, that dancing was an excommunicable offense.[37] Sober church deliverances against other forms of

[34] Methodist Episcopal Church, South, General Conference, *Journal, 1918* (Nashville, n.d.), 490.

[35] Methodist Episcopal Church, South, General Conference, *Journal, 1894,* 34–35.

[36] Southern Baptist Convention, *Annual, 1888* (Atlanta, 1888), 3, 33–34; Greenville, S. C., *Baptist Courier,* May 24, 1888; William W. Barnes, *The Southern Baptist Convention, 1845–1953* (Nashville, 1954), 246. Both Methodists and Baptists vigorously debated the role of their churches in the prohibition movement in the 1880's. The Southern Baptist Convention of 1887 had gone on record in favor of legal prohibition (as had the Southern Methodist General Conference one year earlier). But convention delegates voted to sustain the ruling in 1888.

[37] Presbyterian Church in the United States, General Assembly, *Minutes, 1893* (Richmond, Va., 1893), 35.

"worldliness"—card playing, cursing, Sabbath desecration, gambling, attending theaters, and the like—carried threats of expulsion for such flagrant evidences of apostasy. Local congregations customarily exercised rigorous discipline over their members. But during the immediate post-Civil War years conformity was normally demanded only of church members, and enforcement attempts were confined, in the main, to moral suasion and church discipline.[38] It was the initially hesitant demand for statutory laws upholding some of these codes, and applicable alike to believers and nonbelievers, that brought the southern churches directly into the arena of political agitation. From this limited beginning there came broader condemnations of social ills and, finally, halting assertions of a mission to reform society toward Christian ends. A complaint by the 1902 Southern Presbyterian General Assembly that churches "have been moulded by, rather than helpfully moulded, the spirit of the age" was a harbinger.[39]

Well before the turn of the century, Southern Presbyterians led the way in demanding more stringent blue laws. The 1878 General Assembly called for a "concert of Christian effort to

[38] Hunter Farish finds that before the turn of the century "a major portion of the Southern Methodist efforts at reform were directed against participation in those 'wordly' amusements which, though not specifically condemned by the Scriptures, were yet believed to be conducive to immorality." (Farish, *Circuit Rider Dismounts*, 369.) Rufus B. Spain concludes that, although Southern Baptists during this period "occasionally called for the assistance of government in promoting personal purity laws," they were "usually apathetic toward organized reform movements." (Spain, "Attitudes and Reactions of Southern Baptists," 317, 363.) At the turn of the century the southern churches were yielding in their opposition to some manifestations of worldliness. In 1900 a young Methodist preacher begged Bishop E. R. Hendrix to instruct him on how to administer the *Discipline*'s harsh pronouncements on worldly amusements without creating resentment and disharmony. The bishop replied that "gentleness is needed," that "there are times when silence is golden," and that preachers should "avoid what might be called 'nagging.' " "A manly preacher whose position is already well known from the pulpit is not to be charged with cowardice if he deems it henceforth wise to preach on other themes," the bishop counseled. (Nashville *Christian Advocate*, Jan. 11, 1900.)

[39] Presbyterian Church in the United States, General Assembly, *Minutes, 1902* (Richmond, Va., 1902), 297–98.

abate or remove violations of the holy Sabbath by Sunday railroad trains, steamers, mails, etc.," and commended "legislation of the civil commonwealths" in this area. Again, in 1881, the assembly urged that "Christian people of this country should seek in every lawful way to abate" these evils.[40] Southern Baptists and Methodists withheld their full endorsement from these blue law demands, but they joined Presbyterians before the turn of the century in advocating legal prohibition. The Southern Methodist General Conference condemned the "manufacture, sale, and use of intoxicating liquors, except for medicinal and mechanical purposes" as early as 1886, and pledged to "strive with all good citizens and by all proper and honorable means to banish the horrible evil from our beloved Church and country."[41] A resolution by the Southern Baptist Convention in 1900 summarized the position of that body: "In brief, we favor prohibition for the nation and the State, and total abstinence for the individual, and we believe that no Christian citizen should ever cast a ballot for any man, measure, or platform that is opposed to the annihilation of the liquor traffic." Such specificity also characterized several earlier pronouncements by the convention. The 1887 convention lauded prohibition campaigns then under way in Tennessee and Texas; in 1890 convention delegates endorsed a drive by the "Christian and temperance" people of Atlanta to outlaw "those dens of infamy, the liquor saloons"; and in 1892 the convention congratulated the State of Louisiana "on the destruction of that gigantic engine of Satan—*The Late Louisiana Lottery.*"[42]

Around the turn of the century the southern churches con-

[40] Presbyterian Church in the United States, General Assembly, *Minutes, 1878* (Wilmington, N. C., 1878), 641–42; *Minutes, 1881* (Richmond, Va., 1881), 423.

[41] Methodist Episcopal Church, South, General Conference, *Journal, 1886,* 199.

[42] Southern Baptist Convention, *Annual, 1900* (Nashville, n.d.), 35–36; *Proceedings, 1887* (Atlanta, 1887), 30–31; *Annual, 1890* (Atlanta, 1890), 37; *Annual, 1892* (Atlanta, 1892), 42.

siderably expanded their social interests beyond the limited range of prohibition, gambling, divorce laws, and blue laws. The coming of the new century was in itself a stimulus to reappraisal. Moreover, a slight industrialization in the South contributed to a sense of change, a feeling that old moorings were being lost and that new courses must be charted. Thus the Methodist bishops reflected in 1898:

Standing on the summit of this unparalleled century and casting our glance forward into the next, pregnant with untold possibilities, this General Conference is confronted with extraordinary opportunities, and therefore with momentous responsibilities. God help us to be equal to the times in which we live. . . .

"Long a peaceful, pastoral people, living on farms and villages," the bishops declared in 1906, "we are now rapidly becoming a manufacturing and commercial population, residing in busy towns and crowded cities."[43] The 1903 Presbyterian General Assembly noted that "our Southern land is springing forward in the march of material civilization," and that "this is a critical period in the life of our church."[44] A Southern Baptist committee recalled in 1896 that "our people have been for more than one hundred years mainly a rural people." "Their circumstances have been favorable to the reception of the simple faith of the New Testament," the committee noted. But with changed conditions, "with cities springing up everywhere, we are still pursuing pioneer methods of work. . . ."[45]

Coupled with such observations were demands that the churches lead in shaping new patterns. Declaring that Southern Methodists could not ignore "political, industrial, and social influences that surround us," the bishops proclaimed in 1902 "the mission of the Church to work in these conditions,

[43] Methodist Episcopal Church, South, General Conference, *Journal, 1898* (Nashville, n.d.), 19; *Journal, 1906,* 25.

[44] Presbyterian Church in the United States, General Assembly, *Minutes, 1903* (Richmond, Va., 1903), 505.

[45] Southern Baptist Convention, *Annual, 1896* (Atlanta, 1896), 17–18.

and to bring out of them the results for which the Church o. God was ordained." The narrow sense in which the bishops then construed this mission was illustrated four years later, however, when they expressed compassion for city slum dwellers ("compelled often to live under conditions that produce moral stupor, which becomes practical heathenism") but concluded that "nothing can cleanse and purify these breeding grounds of anarchy and vice but the ethical and vital principles of the gospel."[46] Likewise, the 1908 Southern Baptist Convention resolved that "every wrong, public and private, political and social, retards the consummation of the commission of our King," and that "Christ's commission to his followers is not primarily to increase the census of heaven, but to make down here a righteous society in which Christ's will shall be done, his kingdom come." Yet, having proclaimed these far-reaching principles, the convention proceeded only to rejoice that "politicians today are in increasing numbers consulting with the religious people of the community rather than with the saloon aggregation."[47]

Nevertheless, the authoritative assertion of such principles was portentous. Nor were timely applications unknown. Leaders of all major denominations spoke out against lynching. Methodist editors were especially courageous in this respect.[48] In 1899 the Southern Presbyterian General Assembly condemned lynching as tending "to cheapen human life, to unsettle the social order, and to weaken or destroy that reverence for law and constituted authority which the Scriptures

---

[46] Methodist Episcopal Church, South, General Conference, *Journal*, 1902, 21; *Journal*, 1906, 25.

[47] Southern Baptist Convention, *Annual*, 1908 (Nashville, n.d.), 35–36. General accounts of the rise of the social gospel movement are given in Charles H. Hopkins, *The Rise of the Social Gospel Movement in American Protestantism, 1865–1914* (New Haven, 1940), and Henry F. May, *Protestant Churches and Industrial America* (New York, 1949). The revivalistic origins of social reform are stressed in Timothy L. Smith, *Revivalism and Social Reform in Mid-Nineteenth Century America* (Nashville, 1957).

[48] See Farish, *Circuit Rider Dismounts*, 369.

require all to uphold."[49] The 1906 Southern Baptist Convention declared that "lynching blunts the public conscience, undermines the foundations on which society stands, and if unchecked will result in anarchy." But the Baptists took pains to affirm that "our condemnation is due with equal emphasis, and in many cases with even greater emphasis, against the horrible crimes which cause the lynchings."[50]

More significant were permanent committees and commissions set up to formulate and direct church social reform endeavors. In 1890 the Southern Methodist General Conference designated a Standing Committee on Temperance, to which each annual conference nominated a member. In 1910 this committee was reorganized into a Standing Committee on Temperance and Other Moral and Social Questions.[51] The Southern Baptist Convention created a permanent Committee on Temperance in 1908, instructing it "to promote in every possible way the cause of temperance, until there shall not be a licensed saloon in our land, and until the whole liquor traffic shall be banished not only from our land, but from all lands." In 1913 the convention also established a Social Service Commission "to deal with other such wrongs which curse society today, and call loudly for our help." The committee and the commission were merged the following year to form a Temperance and Social Service Commission.[52] Meanwhile, Southern Methodists and Presbyterians joined Protestant communions throughout the nation in sponsoring the reform-oriented Federal Council of Churches of Christ in America. The council began functioning in 1908, with Southern Methodist Bishop E. R. Hendrix as its first president.[53]

[49] Presbyterian Church in the United States, General Assembly, Minutes, 1899 (Richmond, Va., 1899), 431.
[50] Southern Baptist Convention, Annual, 1906 (Nashville, n.d.), 33.
[51] Methodist Episcopal Church, South, General Conference, Journal, 1890, 150; Journal, 1910 (Nashville, n.d.), 71.
[52] Southern Baptist Convention, Annual, 1908, 36, 48; Annual, 1913, 76; Annual, 1914 (Nashville, n.d.), 38.
[53] Hopkins, Rise of the Social Gospel, 306.

Before America's entry into World War I, Southern Baptists, Methodists, and Presbyterians had all officially espoused broad social reform objectives. The Southern Methodist General Conference incorporated the Social Creed of the Federal Council into its *Book of Discipline,* thereby advocating the regulation of child labor, "the regulation of the conditions of toil of women," "the right of employees and employers alike to organize," a "new emphasis upon the application of Christian principles to the acquisition and use of property and for the most equitable division of the products of industry that can ultimately be devised."[54] Southern Presbyterians did not adopt the creed as a denominational statement, but the 1914 General Assembly did promulgate a milder "United Declaration on Christian Faith and Social Service." This declaration acknowledged the applicability of Christian principles to human societies and affirmed that the churches had "a distinctive work to do in bettering the social relations in this present world." It specifically proclaimed against misuse of child and woman labor, and against wages which were insufficient "to support the man and his family against illness and old age."[55] Although Southern Baptists did not formally adopt a social creed or affiliate with the Federal Council, they did speak out on some of the issues with which the council concerned itself. The 1910 Southern Baptist Convention called for the regulation of child labor; in 1915, the convention's temperance and social service commission condemned sweatshops, the improper use of child and woman labor, crowded tenements, and "heartless greed in corporate wealth and graft in politics." "So long as there is a social inequality, industrial

[54] Methodist Episcopal Church, South, General Conference, *Journal, 1914* (Nashville, n.d.), 249–50.

[55] Presbyterian Church in the United States, General Assembly, *Minutes, 1914* (Richmond, Va., 1914), 28, 162–63. The committee which prepared the declaration represented the (Northern) Presbyterian Church in the United States of America, the United Presbyterian Church of North America, the Associate Reform Synod of the South, and the (Southern) Presbyterian Church in the United States.

injustice, or political crime," the commission declared, "the kingdom of God is not fully come, and you and I have a message and a mission." A year before, the social service commission sought to impress upon local churches that they were "directly responsible for the right solution of social problems," and that they should endeavor to "influence and direct legislation by memorial, protest, and petition, and by the creation of a Christian public opinion. . . ."[56]

When America entered World War I, all three denominations identified our war effort with broad religious-social principles. The Southern Baptist Convention concluded that the issues were not "primarily personal or political," but "in essence religious," touching the "very foundations of the moral law," "concerned with fundamental human rights and liberties." The Southern Methodist General Conference characterized our military effort as a crusade for "liberty, for the rights of the many rather than for the privileges of the few, for the brotherhood of man. . . ." The Southern Presbyterian General Assembly believed that the war was fought for "all things worth having," for the "universal prevalence of the 'righteousness that exalteth a nation.' "[57]

Hence, between the turn of the century and World War I, the three major southern white Protestant groups underwent significant changes in program and outlook. Absorbed at the turn of the century in evangelism and little mindful of social needs beyond blue laws and prohibition, they emerged during the next fifteen years as advocates of social justice, proclaiming the Christian obligation to fashion Christ's kingdom on earth. Of course this awakening of reform interest coincided with the Square Deal, the New Freedom, and the rise of reform

[56] Southern Baptist Convention, Annual, 1910 (Nashville, n.d.), 46–47, 58–59; Annual, 1915 (Nashville, n.d.), 83; Annual, 1914, 36–37.

[57] Southern Baptist Convention, Annual, 1918 (Nashville, n.d.), 74; Methodist Episcopal Church, South, General Conference, Journal, 1918, 99; Presbyterian Church in the United States, General Assembly, Minutes, 1919 (Richmond, Va., 1919), 38, 87.

sentiment nationally. Southern Protestant social pronouncements mirrored the Progressive Movement in tenor and phraseology.[58]

And yet to resolve, to proclaim, and to pronounce was not to strive or to emphasize. Except for prohibition, few social problems received much attention below the level of the conference, the association, or the presbytery. Little beyond the gospel of personal redemption was proclaimed from community pulpits. An exhortation of the Southern Methodist bishops in 1914 was indicative. In expressing compassion for the "fallen and forlorn sons of men," they made it clear that their church

holds them in too high esteem to regard them as no more than animals to be filled with food and satisfied with improved physical conditions . . . she refuses to regard them as hungry brutes to be pampered and pacified with the meat that perisheth, but does rather seek to feed them with the meat that endureth to everlasting life.[59]

Liberal southern Protestants might acknowledge the Christian imperative to reform. But, as ardently as conservatives, they also emphasized spiritual regeneration. On the necessity of this personal commitment there remained a consensus. Justification by faith was the great hope.

---

[58] See, for example, the report of a special Southern Baptist Convention committee on civic righteousness in 1908. (Southern Baptist Convention, *Annual, 1908*, 35–36.) Although the social gospel movement was much weaker in the South than in the North, yet social concern was more manifest among southern religious leaders than has been generally recognized. The evidence does not sustain C. Vann Woodward's tentative conclusion that "the current in the South ran counter" to socialized religion during this period. (Woodward, *Origins of the New South*, 450.)

[59] Methodist Episcopal Church, South, General Conference, *Journal, 1914*, 27–28.

3

FUNDAMENTALISM AND REFORM

$\mathcal{C}$he years following World War I were years of wide disillusionment in the South as throughout the Western world. For many buoyant hopes of the war and pre-war years remained conspicuously unfulfilled—of a new integrity in public life, of social justice and broadening opportunity, of democracy triumphant around the globe. A whirl of technological change contributed to a sense of insecurity. The automobile weakened social controls and induced a veritable revolution in behavior, especially among the younger generation.

It was a time of trial for southern Protestantism. Although the southern churches remained heavily oriented toward evangelism, they had become increasingly identified with social causes in the years before the war. Their endorsements of our war to end wars followed logically from previous reform commitments. Such efforts were poorly vindicated in the era after Versailles. Representative government waned in Europe as wars and rumors of war continued. At home, amidst the Harding scandals and big-time gangsterism, our nation was not exalting itself with righteousness, the Eighteenth Amendment notwithstanding. Rarely had human perversity seemed so utter and appalling.

Many churchmen were dismayed at what the Reverend J. Frank Norris, pastor of the Fort Worth First Baptist Church, damned as "this present godless, commercialized, pleasure-gone-mad, Sabbath-breaking, idol-worshipping, hell-bound age."[1] The Southern Methodist bishops grumbled about "too much of ragtime and too little of psalm." A Southern Presbyterian committee found that "the desire for money, the hunger for pleasure, have overflowed all reasonable bounds and become a positive threat against the very life of the nation." "We have come upon a day," mourned the 1921 Southern Baptist Convention, "when the manifestations of greed and selfishness, and lust for pleasure are so great as to threaten and to rend asunder the entire social fabric, destroy the very foundations of civilization and to plunge the whole world into a withering chasm of unrest and revolution."[2] Of course clerical exhortations against worldliness were not new. But an unusual tone of urgency characterized such pronouncements during the 1920's. For seldom—if ever—had a generation so flouted hallowed traditions and responded so little to censure.

Church councils held several influences especially accountable. The 1926 Southern Baptist Convention proclaimed its "uncompromising disfavor for the salacious and character-destroying [motion] pictures produced and shown the public"; earlier the convention's social service commission concluded

---

[1] Fort Worth *Searchlight*, Mar. 12, 1926.

[2] Methodist Episcopal Church, South, General Conference, *Journal,* 1922 (Nashville, n.d.), 341; Presbyterian Church in the United States, General Assembly, *Minutes,* 1920 (Richmond, Va., 1920), 128; Southern Baptist Convention, *Annual,* 1921 (Nashville, n.d.), 128.

that "the motion picture, as it has been conducted, has served constantly to appeal to and create depraved tastes" and that the industry must either be reformed or banned "as has the liquor traffic." Urging federal censorship, the Southern Methodist General Conference decried "both the private lives of many who are engaged in the making of moving pictures as well as the vile and suggestive pictures which are offered." The automobile's insidious influences were condemned with equal fervor; a Southern Presbyterian committee deplored "unchaperoned automobile riding at night," citing the testimony of a matron of a home for unwed mothers "that a considerable majority of the inmates of her home ascribe their fall to this habit."[3] Some preachers blamed fashions in women's apparel as a major debauching influence. "When the average man ceases to be moved by the shapely limb of the opposite sex," one clergyman exclaimed, "it will be a conclusive argument for sinless perfection, extreme old age or general debility." He speculated that "scant dress is usually accompanied by scant morals" and that "if some of the dresses continue the same ratio for the next twenty-five years that they have maintained for the past ten years, they will be exactly fifteen feet above the head."[4]

No threat to spirituality stirred more vehement protest in the 1920's than dancing. "Accompanied, as it is, by immodest dress, by close physical contact of the sexes, and by its lack of restraint," the Southern Baptist Social Service Commission concluded, "it is undoubtedly doing much to undermine the morals of our young people." A Southern Presbyterian committee cautioned parents that "the public promiscuous dance is the frequent recreation of our high school children" and

[3] Southern Baptist Convention, *Annual*, 1926 (Nashville, n.d.), 114; *Annual*, 1921, 82; Methodist Episcopal Church, South, General Conference, *Journal*, 1926 (Nashville, n.d.), 285; Presbyterian Church in the United States, General Assembly, *Minutes*, 1923 (Richmond, Va., 1923), 84.

[4] John W. Porter, "Dress and Licentiousness," in Memphis *American Baptist*, Feb. 17, 1926, "Dress Reform," *ibid.*, Mar. 3, 1926.

that "young people mixing promiscuously for hours in the modern dance get heated with the exercise and familiar contact. . . ."[5] "There is neither command, example, nor inference that anyone under the Christian dispensation ever attended a dance with the approval of God," opined a contributor to the Church of Christ *Gospel Advocate*.[6] Among the more explicit critics of dancing was the Reverend John W. Porter, pastor of the Lexington, Kentucky, Immanuel Baptist Church and editor of the Memphis *American Baptist*. Porter deplored the modern dance in all its manifestations—"waltz, turkey trot, grizzly bear, bunny hug, buzzard lope and the shimmy, ad nauseam ad infinitum." He complained that dancing usually took place "not, as usually supposed, in 'full evening dress,' but rather in full evening undress," with adultery a "commonplace of the ballroom," and that women often removed their corsets before dancing so that "sexual feelings may be more easily and intensely aroused." Porter was sure there was "more of lust, fornication, and adultery than at any period in the world's civilized history."[7]

A doleful picture it was. But what lessons did these unhappy trends hold for southern Protestantism? On this there was vigorous debate. As international relations deteriorated, most religious leaders came to believe that church endorsements of our participation in World War I were mistaken. Implied recantations came from the highest denominational sources during the 1920's. The Southern Baptist Convention resolved emphatically that "war is contrary to the spirit and teaching of Jesus Christ, and that it is the greatest obstacle to the progress of Christianity"; the Southern Methodist General Conference pledged itself to stand "steadfastly against the

[5] Southern Baptist Convention, *Annual*, 1921, 83; Presbyterian Church in the United States, General Assembly, *Minutes*, 1921 (Richmond, Va., 1921), 61; *Minutes*, 1923, 84.

[6] L. L. Yeagley, "Dancing," in Nashville *Gospel Advocate*, Apr. 5, 1928.

[7] Memphis *American Baptist*, Jan. 20, Mar. 3, 30, 1926. Earlier in the 1920's, Porter had been pastor of the Lexington First Baptist Church.

further recurrence of the military mania" as it urged communicants to "loathe war and hate war, and strip it of all its
falseness and glamour and let it stand forth in its unveiled
hideousness"; the Southern Presbyterian General Assembly
proclaimed that "the Church should never again bless a war,
or be used as an instrument in the promotion of war."[8] There
was likewise general agreement on another vital previous involvement; few dedicated Protestants openly challenged the
role their churches had assumed in the prohibition movement.
But beyond these two spheres—war and prohibition—there
was little consensus on past performances or present needs.

Militant factions in all the popular churches demanded
drastic curtailments of reform endeavors and an expanded
evangelistic emphasis. This viewpoint was well expressed in a
resolution adopted by the Southern Baptist Convention in
1921. The resolution declared it "fully demonstrated in the
times in which we live that nothing but the power of the
gospel in regeneration of individual men in large numbers can
ever make the world safe for the highest happiness and most
real peace. . . ."[9] Such statements were often coupled with
definitions of dogma. Abhorring "modernism," religious conservatives clamored for a return to "fundamental" precepts
and polity. An unchanging, infallible Bible was the bedrock
of their faith. Indeed the greater the accumulation of evidence
discrediting a full literal acceptance of the Scriptures, the
more ardently did fundamentalists champion the Word as it
stood. Though the fundamentalist movement was national

[8] Southern Baptist Convention, *Annual, 1924* (Nashville, n.d.), 81; Methodist Episcopal Church, South, General Conference, *Journal, 1926*, 301;
Presbyterian Church in the United States, General Assembly, *Minutes, 1929*
(Richmond, Va., 1929), 80. Despite such resolutions, the southern churches
loaned their general support to our efforts in World War II and during the
military action in Korea. But they did not identify these wars so fully with
divine purpose, nor were their expectations of accomplishments so exaggerated
as in World War I.

[9] Southern Baptist Convention, *Annual, 1921*, 28.

and international in scope, the American South was the region of its greatest vitality.[10]

A concerted campaign stemmed from a Conference on Christian Fundamentals which met in Philadelphia in 1919. Warning against a great apostasy "spreading like a plague through Christendom," the conference deliberated and mapped strategy. In its published program, entitled *God Hath Spoken*, procedures were outlined to ferret out modernism root and branch: to compile a definitive bibliography of "sound" religious books, to extend the conservative influence over the religious press, to identify "such colleges, seminaries and academies as refuse to use text books or employ teachers that undermine faith in the Bible," to work for the recall of unorthodox missionaries, and to sponsor conservative Bible study conferences throughout the land. The conference organized a World's Christian Fundamentals Association to carry out this ambitious program. "The future will look back on the World Conference on Christian Fundamentals . . . as an event of more historical moment than the nailing up, at Wittenberg, of Martin Luther's ninety-five theses," one speaker predicted.[11] Numerous kindred organizations also marshaled for action, including the Antievolution League of America, the Supreme Kingdom, and the Florida-based Bible Crusaders of America. A similar tone and temper characterized them all. In a bombastic call to arms, rendered "in the name of Christ

[10] The standard treatment of the fundamentalist controversy in America during the 1920's is Norman F. Furniss, *The Fundamentalist Controversy, 1918–1931* (New Haven, 1954). An older, less satisfactory study is Stewart G. Cole, *The History of Fundamentalism* (New York, 1931). Louis Gasper, *The Fundamentalist Movement* (The Hague, 1962) deals with the movement in American Protestantism since 1930. None of these works give adequate attention to conflicts between fundamentalist and liberal factions in the southern churches.

[11] World Conference on Christian Fundamentals, *God Hath Spoken* (Philadelphia, 1919), 7–8, 13, 10–11, 20–23, 27. See also Marie Acomb Riley, *The Dynamics of a Dream: The Life of Dr. William B. Riley* (Grand Rapids, 1938), 123.

and the Bible," Bible Crusader George F. Washburn proclaimed: "I now, . . . as Director General of the Bible Crusaders of America, appeal to the 80 million Fundamentalists of America to stand as a solid phalanx against the Satanic invasion of rationalism and infidelity that is sweeping over the nation." The challenge to religious liberalism was real—and indeed to the very existence of the established Protestant bodies. "The creeds of fundamentalists, even of different denominations, . . . are much nearer agreement than the creeds of fundamentalists and modernists in the same denomination," the *Crusader's Champion* observed.[12]

Less than a half-dozen leaders tended to dominate the movement on the national and international level. Chief among them was William Bell Riley, pastor of the Minneapolis First Baptist Church, editor of the *Christian Fundamentalist*, and long-time president of the World's Christian Fundamentals Association. William Jennings Bryan eulogized Riley as "the greatest statesman in the American pulpit";[13] the Louisville *Western Recorder* doubted whether "Baptists or others have produced in this generation his equal as a conservative exponent of Christian faith in a day of unbelief."[14] "His mind is as keen as the blade of Saladin and as powerful as the sword of Richard the Lion Hearted," one admirer marveled.[15] In the forefront with Riley was the Reverend T. T. Shields, pastor of the Toronto Jarvis Street Baptist Church, editor of the *Gospel Witness*, and president both of the Toronto Baptist Theological Seminary and of the Baptist Bible Union of North America. An observer sized up Shields as "inflexible of will, domineering, the very incarnation of fanat-

[12] Memphis *American Baptist*, April 21, 1926; *Crusader's Champion*, quoted *ibid.*, June 30, 1926.
[13] Fort Worth *Searchlight*, May 14, 1926.
[14] Louisville *Western Recorder*, quoted in Fort Worth *Fundamentalist*, Sept. 18, 1931.
[15] Fort Worth *Searchlight*, May 14, 1926. Riley, *Dynamics of a Dream*, is an authorized biography prepared by the clergyman's wife.

ical conviction."[16] Also in the conservative vanguard was the Reverend John Roach Straton, pastor of the Calvary Baptist Church in New York City. Straton's fiery altercations brought him frequently into the national limelight. In January 1924, before a capacity crowd at Carnegie Hall, he argued the negative in a debate over whether "the Earth and Man came by Evolution."[17]

In Forth Worth, the Reverend J. Frank Norris directed his unrivaled vituperative talents against those he assailed as betrayers of the faith. Riley, Shields, Straton, and Norris worked closely together. "Should it be thought a thing incredible," Norris boasted in 1928, "the marvelous blessings of grace that at this present time are being poured out upon four churches . . . which have been storm centers—Jarvis Street, Toronto; First Baptist, Minneapolis; Calvary, New York; and the First Baptist Church, Fort Worth?" Among southern Protestant leaders Norris had few peers. His church was asserted to be the largest religious congregation in the world. His sermons were carried to as many as 100,000 subscribers of the *Searchlight*. And he broadcast regularly over a radio station which he owned. "I know of no man in my world-wide acquaintance who stands in such a position of power as Norris occupies this moment," William Bell Riley exclaimed in 1931.[18] Although these four key clerical leaders were all Baptists, at least one Presbyterian and one Methodist clergyman played active roles at the Philadelphia conference.[19]

William Jennings Bryan probably did most to popularize

[16] "The Fundamentalist Fiasco," *Christian Century*, XLVI (1929), 672.

[17] New York *Times*, Jan. 29, 1924. For press accounts of Shields and Straton see *ibid.*, Dec. 29, 1923, May 14, Nov. 11, 1927, Apr. 15, 1928, Oct. 30, 1929.

[18] Fort Worth *Fundamentalist*, Feb. 10, 1928, Feb. 20, 1931. The *Searchlight* became the *Fundamentalist* on Apr. 15, 1927.

[19] The Reverend A. B. Winchester, pastor of the Knox Presbyterian Church, Toronto, Canada, and the Reverend L. W. Munhall, editor of the *Eastern Methodist*, were on the program at the Philadelphia conference. (*God Hath Spoken*, 123–40, 361–93.)

the movement. Until his death in 1925, Bryan campaigned tirelessly "to save the Christian Church from those who are trying to destroy her faith."[20] His status among religious conservatives was reminiscent of his earlier standing in the councils of the Democratic party. Though a passionate and fiery advocate, the Commoner exercised greater restraint than many others. For he crusaded with some who were little but troublemakers, perennial heresy hunters, men whose lust for conflict and power seemed often paramount. Such men and such a movement flourished in a climate which also produced the Great Red Scare and the rejuvenated Ku-Klux Klan.[21]

All major white southern churches felt the impact of the movement, although its effects in the Presbyterian Church in the United States were slight. The 1923 General Assembly admonished synods "to exercise a zealous care over all the schools under their control, to see that no teacher occupies a chair in any one of these schools whose religious views are not in harmony with the evangelical doctrines of our faith." And the assembly the following year reaffirmed that "Adam's body was directly fashioned by Almighty God without any natural animal parentage of any kind out of matter previously created from nothing. . . ."[22] This dogma was the basis of charges brought in 1929 against the Reverend Hay Watson

[20] New York *Times*, May 19, 1923. Bryan's role in the fundamentalist movement is treated in Paxton Hibben, *The Peerless Leader, William Jennings Bryan* (New York, 1929), Morris R. Werner, *Bryan* (New York, 1929), and Mary Baird Bryan and William Jennings Bryan, *The Memoirs of William Jennings Bryan* (Chicago, 1925).

[21] For a perceptive treatment of the Red Scare and the Klan, see Frederick Lewis Allen, *Only Yesterday: An Informal History of the Nineteen-Twenties* (New York, 1952), 40–67.

[22] Presbyterian Church in the United States, General Assembly, *Minutes, 1923,* 60; *Minutes, 1924* (Richmond, Va., 1924), 64. A convenient brief history of the Presbyterian Church in the United States is given in Walter L. Lingle, *Presbyterians: Their History and Beliefs* (Richmond, 1956). The publication of Volume II of Ernest Trice Thompson, *Presbyterians in the South* (2 vols, Richmond, 1963–   ), will provide a more extensive treatment. The appearance of this volume, covering the period from 1861 to present, is expected soon.

Smith, pastor of the Little Rock Second Presbyterian Church. An admitted Darwinist, Smith also agitated for a "recasting of some parts of the older theology," "greater freedom and courage in the pursuit of truth," and honest acknowledgment that the Bible was not literally without error.[23] When the Arkansas Presbytery refused to condemn him as a heretic, appeals were made to the Arkansas Synod and to the General Assembly. Undeterred by Smith's aspersions on "the stupidity and ridiculousness of all heresy hunting," his accusers continued to press charges until his case had been deliberated four times by the Arkansas Presbytery, three times by the Arkansas Synod, and four times by the General Assembly. Finally, in 1934, with Smith still uncensured, the General Assembly resolved to "decline to consider further overtures from any source regarding this case."[24]

Southern Methodists were plagued by more serious frictions. Amidst conservative grumblings, the 1922 General Conference expressed cautious gratification that "our educational institutions, despite adverse criticism, are loyal to the idea of teaching the Bible as the authorized Word of God." But the 1926 conference adopted a fundamentalist-phrased resolution exhorting "all ministers and laymen to guard against all sinister influences, false doctrines, and compromises which would result in loss of faith and purity of life."[25] The church had few rigid doctrines, however, and its bishops made no effort to compel a narrow conformity. The articulation of opposing viewpoints was well illustrated when the issue of antievolution laws arose. After the Southern Methodist Educational Association deplored "all legislation that would interfere with the

[23] Hay Watson Smith, *Evolution and Presbyterianism* (Little Rock, 1922), 14, 81.
[24] Presbyterian Church in the United States, General Assembly, *Minutes*, 1929, 82–83; *Minutes*, 1930 (Richmond, Va., 1930), 41; *Minutes*, 1933 (Richmond, 1933), 58; *Minutes*, 1934 (Richmond, 1934), 43–45; New York *Times*, June 29, 1931.
[25] Methodist Episcopal Church, South, General Conference, *Journal*, 1922, 289; *Journal*, 1926, 213.

proper teaching of scientific subjects in American schools and colleges," a Mississippi quarterly conference voted to "repudiate and condemn the action of the Education Association in this matter" and to "withdraw our support from any Methodist school or college that teaches or permits to be taught any scientific subject which is contrary to the teaching of the Holy Scriptures."[26] In the Southwest a controversy arose over the allegedly modernistic teachings of John A. Rice, a professor at Southern Methodist University. Fundamentalists demanded his dismissal. When Rice "graciously and on his own volition" tendered his resignation, it was accepted by the university, to the dismay of academic liberals on the faculty.[27]

Two questions provoked serious divisions between liberal and conservative factions in the Southern Methodist General Conference. One question involved the educational preparation of preachers. Traditionally no formal schooling was required for ordination into the Southern Methodist ministry, though unschooled preachers had to complete home study courses in theology and religion. But a rule first adopted in 1914 and slightly amended four years later established a high school education as a minimum, except "that under special conditions clearly recognized as unusual, the Annual Conference may by a two-thirds vote admit a candidate who does not meet the academic requirements." In 1926 a General Conference committee recommended that the ordinary minimum standard be raised to two years of college work, and that exception by two-thirds annual conference vote be tolerated only when a candidate had at least completed a secondary education.[28]

[26] Nashville *Christian Advocate*, Apr. 1, 15, 1927; "The 'Spirit of Wesley' in the South," in *Literary Digest*, Mar. 19, 1927.

[27] Hiram Abiff Boaz, *Eighty-four Golden Years: An Autobiography* (Nashville, 1951), 111. Boaz was president of Southern Methodist University at the time of the controversy.

[28] Methodist Episcopal Church, South, *Doctrines and Discipline, 1914* (Nashville, 1914), 287–88; *Doctrines and Discipline, 1918* (Nashville, 1918), 309; General Conference, *Daily Christian Advocate, 1926* (Nashville, 1926), 55. Indian and Mexican preachers were excluded from these requirements.

The proposal to exclude without exception all those who were not high school graduates was hotly debated. "Let us remember that we cannot control God," Asbury College President H. C. Morrison declared. Morrison argued that the rule would "shut out droves of young men with limited education" who were "called" to preach, men who were "spirit-filled and God-filled and on fire" and who were "getting people saved." One delegate grumbled that such stringency would exclude "every apostle that Jesus Christ called into the ministry"; another complained that this "would make Southern Methodism a high-brow church." Advocates of the change warned that "we are filling our Conferences with men who do not measure up to the standard," that existing regulations did not preclude annual conferences from accepting ministers who had as little as "a fourth grade education or a sixth grade education or a third grade education." "Your Committee on Education is seeking to put a bottom into a bottomless bucket," a spokesman explained. But by a margin of 195 to 166 the General Conference voted to retain the bottomless bucket. The stipulated minimum requirement was raised to junior college graduation, but no level was established below which exception could not be made by two-thirds vote of an annual conference.[29]

More serious than the conflict over educational standards, however, was a cleavage which arose over a movement toward reunification with Northern Methodism. Doctrine and orthodoxy were involved; but race relations was apparently the more important issue. As early as 1911 a unification proposal was drawn up by a commission representing both churches.

[29] Methodist Episcopal Church, South, General Conference, *Daily Christian Advocate*, 1926, 94; *Journal*, 1926, 194–95. The General Conference of 1934 prescribed the completion of four years of satisfactory college work as the ordinary minimum educational requirement for ordination into the clergy; exception by two-thirds vote of an annual conference would henceforth be tolerated only when the candidate had completed two years in college. (Methodist Episcopal Church, South, General Conference, *Journal*, 1934 [Nashville, 1934], 104.)

Under this initial plan, northern and southern annual conferences would organize under one general conference and
several intermediate "jurisdictional" conferences. One jurisdictional conference would be comprised of Negro congregations in the northern church "and such other organizations
of colored Methodists as may enter into agreement with
them." The Southern Methodist General Conference in 1914
voted "in favor" of the merger but asked that "the colored
membership of the various Methodist bodies be formed into
an independent organization." Two years later the Northern
General Conference added its endorsement but, "conforming
to the suggestion of the Joint Commission," insisted that "the
colored membership of the reorganized church be constituted
into one or more Quadrennial or Jurisdictional Conferences."
It was thus clear that agreement had yet to be reached on
whether Negroes in the northern church were to be admitted
into the reunited body.[30]

The joint commission continued its tedious deliberations
and in 1920 submitted a second plan which dealt more explicitly with race. The commissioners now recommended one
general conference, six regional white jurisdictions, and one
national all-Negro jurisdiction. Representation from the Negro
jurisdiction could not exceed 5 per cent of the total in any
general conference. Observing that "there appears to be in
each church considerable numbers who are not entirely satisfied with the plan," the northern church rejected it soon after
it was submitted.[31]

Negotiations continued, however, and in 1924 the commis-

[30] Methodist unification efforts are treated in John M. Moore, *The Long
Road to Methodist Union* (New York, 1943); a résumé of previous efforts
appears in (Northern) Methodist Episcopal Church, General Conference,
Daily Christian Advocate, 1920 (Des Moines, 1920) 58–62. Racial segregation
as a barrier to unification is discussed in Dwight W. Culver, *Negro Segregation
in The Methodist Church* (New Haven, 1953), 60–78.

[31] Methodist Episcopal Church, General Conference, *Daily Christian Advocate, 1920*, 432, 439. The text of this unification plan is given in Moore,
Methodist Union, 149–60.

sioners proposed yet another framework. This third scheme would constitute the southern and northern churches as two autonomous jurisdictions loosely federated through a general conference. A key provision required that "every vote in the General Conference shall be by Jurisdictions and shall require the accepted majority vote of each Jurisdiction to be effective." Although the bishops would organize into one "College," each of the two major jurisdictions would elect its own bishops; no bishop could serve outside the jurisdiction which chose him except by invitation of a majority of the bishops in the other jurisdiction. White Southern Methodists would commingle with Negro co-religionists only in the general conference and in the college of bishops. Negro participation in these bodies would be by way of the predominantly white northern jurisdiction.[32]

Northern Methodists approved this plan with little dissent, the General Conference by vote of 802 to 12, the various annual conferences by an 18,140 to 935 majority. But southern reaction was less enthusiastic. Nineteen southern members of the joint commission subscribed to the report; four others refused. The nonsigners issued a statement lamenting that Negro bishops "would be treated exactly like white bishops," that "they may be elected to preside over the meetings of the College of Bishops," and that such fraternization would "weaken the foundations of our social structure and impair the fabric of Southern civilization."[33]

Opponents of union were astutely led by Bishop Warren A. Candler. Assailing the northern church (and its two Negro bishops specifically) for modernistic tendencies, he termed the merger proposal a "Trojan horse filled with men and arms of

[32] The text of the plan appears in Methodist Episcopal Church, South, General Conference, *Daily Christian Advocate, 1924* (Chattanooga, 1924), 20, and in Moore, *Methodist Union,* 169–73.
[33] (Northern) Methodist Episcopal Church, General Conference, *Journal, 1928* (Chicago, 1928), 1681–82; Methodist Episcopal Church, South, General Conference, *Daily Christian Advocate, 1924,* 37.

war." It was "too clear to deny with any show of reason that the Churches of the South must save the cause of evangelical Christianity in the United States or it will be lost," he asserted.[34] Candler invoked political and social as well as religious arguments. He scorned northern Bible critics and educators—"men tainted with these hurtful 'isms' "—for advocating "sociological porous plasters to draw out of human hearts the virus of sin"; he feared that if the influence of such people continued to grow, "the Federal government will become a tyrannical Socialism engaged in extorting money from all the people in order to make appropriations to some of the people." He was convinced that "the welfare of the entire country is involved in the maintenance of evangelical Christianity in the South."[35]

An emotional debate erupted at a special session of the Southern Methodist General Conference which convened in 1924. "There could not be a more grave crime against the negro race," one speaker averred, "than for us to yield the point our fathers made that there shall never be social equality between the races south of the Mason and Dixon line." "The Southern people have decided definitely, and finally and irrevocably," declared another speaker, "that it is best for the negro, that it is best for the white man, that it is best for the civilization that has built up in this Southern land that these two races should not be brought into contact . . . on terms of equality." "Do you object to this plan," a delegate asked, "because Northern Methodists do not approve the Jim Crow law? Would they have to approve it before you endorse any plan?" President Charles C. Selecman of Southern Methodist University pleaded for unification. Selecman felt that the choice was whether to "swing out into a bigger destiny, with broader affiliations and sympathies, or be shut up to the destiny of a narrow and narrowing provincialism." "We may

[34] Nashville *Christian Advocate*, Aug. 15, 1924, Jan. 30, 1925.
[35] *Ibid.*, June 6, 1924, Feb. 12, 1926, Nov. 4, 1927.

just as well confess it," he declared, "that a radical conservatism in politics is bad, a radical conservatism in society is worse, but the worst kind of radical conservatism that has cursed the world and has divided our Christian Church is the radical ecclesiastical conservatism to the voice of which we are to listen here today."[36]

The General Conference voted its approval 297 to 75. But the concurrence of three-fourths of all delegates attending Southern Methodist annual conferences was also required for final ratification. And this last procedure brought defeat to the plan. The aggregate vote of the annual conferences was 4,528 to 4,108 for merger, but this was far short of the necessary majority. Acknowledging this verdict, the 1926 General Conference called for a cessation of all "agitation, discussion or negotiations concerning unification during the ensuing quadrennium."[37] "Postponement of the unification issue at the Methodist Conference is construed by General Washburn [of the Bible Crusaders of America] as a victory for the fundamentalists," the *Crusader's Champion* announced, "it being their purpose to prevent unification of the Methodist Episcopal Church, South, with the more modernistic northern branch of Methodism."[38]

Southern Baptists too were rent by unusual conservative-liberal frictions during the 1920's. Of course the Baptists were not a "Church" in the usual sense, but rather thousands of independent local churches loosely associated for limited common purposes. Although congregations designated official Messengers to district and state associations, and to the annual Southern Baptist Convention, no coercive authority was delegated to these bodies. Support of all programs was voluntary.

[36] Methodist Episcopal Church, South, General Conference, *Daily Christian Advocate*, 1924, 27, 28, 32.

[37] Official reports of this unsuccessful unification attempt appear in Methodist Episcopal Church, South, General Conference, *Journal*, 1926, 316–17, and (Northern) Methodist Episcopal Church, General Conference, *Journal*, 1928, 1681–82.

[38] Quoted in Memphis *American Baptist*, June 30, 1926.

But Baptist co-operative activities had steadily expanded over the years. A Sunday School Board, a Foreign Mission Board, and three theological seminaries were major institutions sponsored by the Southern Baptist Convention. State associations sponsored weekly papers, hospitals, orphanages, colleges, and miscellaneous other enterprises. Such agencies exerted an influence over the denomination that was more real than apparent. They did much to unify, but they inevitably became objects of strife when conflicts over doctrine developed.[39]

Conservative Baptists were more identified with the fundamentalist movement *per se* than conservative factions in most denominations; and they were prone to demand endorsement of their positions as a *sine qua non* for their support of denominational programs. William Bell Riley was a powerful influence among them. Although a Northern Baptist, he was an alumnus of the Southern Baptist Theological Seminary and an active participant in Southern Baptist affairs. "We would prefer," he proclaimed in 1928, "that Baptist history stopped at this point, and that the denomination were never heard of again in human history, than that its glorious past would simply prove to have been the construction of churches and schools, and the establishment of missions, and the erection of publication societies for the final occupation of Unitarians."[40]

But Southern Baptist fundamentalists had their own high priest in J. Frank Norris. Driven by strong animosities toward those with whom he differed, Norris crusaded perennially against apostasy and malfeasance in high places. Three times

[39] The co-operative program was enlarged as a result of a concerted campaign from 1919 to 1924 to raise $75,000,000.00 ($58,591,713.69 was actually collected). In 1917 the Southern Baptist Convention designated an executive committee to oversee denominational enterprises on a continuing basis; an executive secretary was appointed in 1927. (Barnes, *Southern Baptist Convention*, 178–79, 223–24.)

[40] Fort Worth *Fundamentalist*, Jan. 6, 1928. An excellent discussion of the fundamentalist controversy among Southern Baptists is given in William Owen Carver, *Out of His Treasure* (Nashville, 1956), 77–87.

during his turbulent career he was indicted on felonious charges and three times acquitted. The first two indictments were for arson and perjury following the burning of his church in 1912. The third indictment, in 1926, was for murder.[41]

Norris' murder indictment was a national sensation, coming as it did amidst his campaign of denunciation against the Fort Worth city administration. In a Sunday sermon on July 11, 1926, delivered before his congregation, broadcast over radio station KFQB, and published in the *Searchlight*, Norris scorned Mayor H. C. Meacham and his associates as a "two by four, simlin-headed, sawdust-brained, bunch of grafters." He alluded to the city manager as "that missing link." "I am not going to reflect on the Mayor's character," he sneered, "for a man has got to have one before it can be reflected on." Ominously, he accused unidentified parties of "tampering with the wires" of his radio station and served notice that "some of you low down devils that monkey around this property, arrange for your undertaker before you come around here." His guards would "shoot to kill," he told his applauding listeners.[42]

Six days later a friend of Mayor Meacham's—D. C. Chipps —remonstrated with Norris in the clergyman's study. During the argument that ensued, Norris snatched a pistol from his desk and fired four shots. Chipps fell to the floor fatally wounded. Although the victim was unarmed, officials of Norris' church sought to implicate him with a "diabolical conspiracy" to murder their pastor.[43] Norris won court acquittal on a plea of self-defense, claiming that his victim threatened him verbally and made gestures as if to produce a weapon. "To regret an act is one thing," he asserted, "and to regret the necessity that was forced upon you is wholly a different thing." "I say, a man when he is forced and compelled

[41] A summary of Norris' career appeared in the New York *Times*, Jan. 13, 1929.
[42] Fort Worth *Searchlight*, July 16, 1926.
[43] New York *Times*, July 18, 20, 1926.

to face that crisis [such as he had faced] if he plays the part of the sulking coward he is unworthy of the respect of all men and women everywhere."[44] On the day following the killing, he conducted his regular Sunday morning service. His text was Romans 8:1: "There is therefore now no condemnation to them which are in Christ Jesus, who walk not after the flesh, but after the Spirit."[45]

The lack of restraint which culminated in the fatal encounter with Chipps also characterized Norris' relations with fellow clergymen. He castigated "leaders of the Baptist denomination" for saying that "they don't believe in the verbal inspiration" and scorned the Texas Baptist "machine" for condoning "rationalist rot." Typical headlines in his paper proclaimed that "INVESTIGATION NOT ONLY CONFIRMS BAYLOR MEDICAL COLLEGE PROFESSOR CATHOLIC BUT EDUCATED FOR ROMAN CATHOLIC PRIEST"; "DEMAND OF AN OVERWHELMING MAJORITY OF SOUTHERN BAPTISTS TO ELIMINATE THE EDUCATION BOARD, HOSPITALS AND OTHER UNSCRIPTURAL AND MODERNISTIC INSTITUTIONS"; and "REVOLT AGAINST ECCLESIASTICAL DICTATION AMONG BAPTISTS SPREADING RAPIDLY."[46] Interspersed with such attacks were complaints of persecutions by the leaders of the Southern Baptist Convention and the Baptist General Convention of Texas. "The methods of persecution pursued by the Jesuits and the torture of the Spanish Inquisition were merciful," he lamented, "when compared with the persecution at the hands of present-day modernists and ecclesiastical tyrants."[47]

Joining often with Norris was a well-known coterie of Southern Baptist conservatives. Few clergymen in America gave such single-minded emphasis to religious apostasy as the Reverend Mordecai F. Hamm, itinerant evangelist and one-

[44] Forth Worth *Searchlight*, Sept. 17, 1926.
[45] *Ibid.*, July 23, 1926.
[46] Fort Worth *Fundamentalist*, July 1, 1927, Mar. 30, 1928, Oct. 18, Dec. 6, 1929.
[47] Fort Worth *Searchlight*, May 7, 1926.

time pastor of the Oklahoma City First Baptist Church (Hamm's promoters advertised that more than 230,000 had been converted or "reclaimed" at services conducted by him prior to 1930).[48] The Reverend John W. Porter was equally obsessed with the menace of modernism, as was the Reverend H. Boyce Taylor, pastor of the Murray, Kentucky, First Baptist Church and editor of *News and Truth*, and the Reverend Thomas T. Martin, Baptist evangelist and professor at Blue Mountain (Mississippi) College.

Their attack centered especially on denominational colleges and universities; "many of our Baptist schools are only Baptist in name," Porter grumbled.[49] Presidents and professors were badgered incessantly for statements on controversial points. "Do you believe," a Baptist editor queried President E. Y. Mullins of the Southern Baptist Theological Seminary, "that God created man in the beginning with a body practically like he has today, by an immediate act, and not by any process of evolution or development from a lower form?"[50] Mullins admonished one such inquisitor that "some of you brethren who train with the radical fundamentalists are going over on Catholic ground and leaving the Baptist position. . . . A man who tries to pin his brethren down to stereotyped statements, such as your letter contains, has missed the Baptist spirit."[51] A professor at the Louisville seminary rebuked an accuser for "representing me as believing and teaching what I have declared I do not believe or teach; and what I am convinced that you do not yourself think that I believe or teach." The professor wondered how fundamentalists knew "what books were dangerous, and how did it happen that they could read them safely while the rest of us could not."[52] In 1922 President S. P.

---

[48] Fort Worth *Fundamentalist*, Jan. 10, 1930.
[49] Memphis *American Baptist*, Dec. 16, 1925.
[50] The question was asked by C. P. Stealey, editor of the Oklahoma City *Baptist Messenger*, and quoted in Fort Worth *Searchlight*, Apr. 9, 1926.
[51] *Ibid.*, Apr. 16, 1926.
[52] Carver, *Out of His Treasure*, 83, 87.

Brooks of Baylor University was summoned before the Baptist General Convention of Texas to defend his institution against charges that Darwinism was taught there.[53]

Fundamentalists were probably more firmly entrenched among the Baptists of Kentucky than in any other state. The state Baptist association voted in 1922 to ban the theory of evolution from schools which it supported;[54] three years later denominational support of Cumberland College was suspended when Cumberland officials declined to dismiss a professor who was accused of pro-Darwinian tendencies. Campbellsville College was more compliant. Campbellsville trustees directed faculty members to subscribe to a statement condemning the theory of evolution and affirming that "we believe that the greatest menace to truth and spiritual religion are rationalism, destructive criticism and the substitution of culture and social service for personal regeneration through the operation of the Holy Spirit; that these teachings are contrary to God's Word, discredit the teachings of Jesus, deny His deity and are destructive to the foundations of Christianity and civilization."[55]

For several years a fierce struggle raged in the Southern Baptist Convention between fundamentalists and more moderately oriented elements; indeed the cleavage seemed as serious as the Whitsitt-Landmark controversy in the late nineteenth century.[56] Fundamentalists demanded that the convention adopt precise standards of orthodoxy against which false teachers and preachers might be judged. In 1924 the convention designated a special committee to consider such action. Under the chairmanship of E. Y. Mullins the com-

[53] New York *Times*, Nov. 18, 1922.
[54] *Ibid.*, Nov. 18, 1922.
[55] Murray, Kentucky, *News and Truth*, June 17, Sept. 2, 1925.
[56] Lynn E. May, Jr., "Baptist Theological Battles are Not New," in Nashville *Baptist and Reflector*, Oct. 18, 1962, is an able summary of the more serious controversies which have arisen among Southern Baptists.

mittee proceeded to draft a lengthy Statement of Baptist Faith and Message which it submitted for final approval the next year. Although presented as "a reaffirmation of Christian fundamentals," the statement was not explicit enough to meet the demands of more ardent conservatives. An effort from the floor to add an unequivocal refutation of the Darwinian theory failed by vote of 2103 to 930. The convention then approved the report as originally drafted as its "consensus of opinion."[57] The authority of the convention was limited to the boards, agencies, and seminaries which it sponsored; state and district associations, and local congregations, could adopt or disregard the statement as they saw fit.

Fundamentalists were also greatly disturbed by a statement issued in 1925 by the Southern Baptist Educational Association, an organization of denominational school educators. Proclaiming that the "Bible cannot be taken literally and never was meant to be," the educators cautioned church colleges to "avoid alliance with either Fundamentalism or Modernism and strive to bring them together on a working basis." "A COLLEGE THAT WILL 'AVOID ALLIANCE' WITH THE TEACHING THAT THE BIBLE IS THE WORD OF GOD . . . HAS NO RIGHT TO GO TO HONEST BAPTISTS FOR THEIR MONEY," retorted the Reverend Thomas T. Martin. Indeed Martin was now convinced that a breakup of the Southern Baptist Convention must follow. "The God of the Fundamentalist is one God," he wrote; "the God of the Modernist is another." "Let us," he asked,

by vote of the Convention, agree to divide peaceably in this way: Let all who endorse this action, this stand taken by the Southern Baptist Educational Association, go into one Convention; let all who reject and repudiate this action go into the other Convention.

Let the proposition be submitted to every church in the

[57] Southern Baptist Convention, *Annual, 1925* (Nashville, n.d.), 71–75; Nashville *Tennessean*, May 15, 1925. See Robert G. Torbet, *A History of the Baptists* (Chicago, 1963), 431.

Southern Baptist Convention; to every college, to every denominational paper; to every pastor; to every evangelist; to every church on foreign fields, to every missionary.

If this were not done, he warned, "there is going to be fearful division and strife."[58]

But the quarrel soon subsided. Most conservatives were mollified by actions taken in the 1926 Southern Baptist Convention. By unanimous vote that body resolved that "this Convention accepts Genesis as teaching that man was the special creation of God, and rejects every theory, evolution or other, which teaches that man originated in, or came by way of, a lower animal ancestry." The convention then requested missionaries, boards, and institutions under its control to signify a "hearty and individual acceptance of the said action of the Convention to the end that the great cause of our present unrest and agitation over the Evolution question may be effectively and finally removed in the minds of the constituency of the Convention and all others concerned."[59] Cries of elation arose from the fundamentalists. In banner headlines Norris' *Searchlight* proclaimed that "SOUTHERN BAPTIST CONVENTION HEROICALLY AND TRIUMPHANTLY DELIVERS KNOCKOUT BLOW AGAINST EVOLUTION AND EVOLUTIONISTS." Porter's *American Baptist* rejoiced that the "evolution question has been satisfactorily disposed of" and admonished Baptists now to "study the things that make for peace."[60] The price of unity was a straightforward disavowal of modernism. Perhaps in no major Protestant denomination in America did conservatives reign more triumphantly.

Victory tended sharply to divide Baptist conservatives into loyalist and secessionist factions. For as extremists continued their familiar calls to arms, it became increasingly apparent

[58] Thomas T. Martin, "A Proposal to Divide the Southern Baptist Convention," in Murray, Kentucky, *News and Truth*, Apr. 1, 1925.

[59] Southern Baptist Convention, *Annual*, 1926, 18, 98.

[60] Fort Worth *Searchlight*, May 21, 1926; Memphis *American Baptist*, June 2, 1926.

that their purpose was more to disrupt than to purify. During the late 1920's and early 1930's, Southern Baptist loyalists took pains to dissociate themselves from interdenominational fundamentalists, and particularly from J. Frank Norris.

As early as 1926 John W. Porter assailed a proposal to organize a new Fundamentalist Church as a "fulfillment of prophecy concerning the Great Apostasy." "We are, to be sure, a 'fundamentalist' as opposed to the 'modernist,' but not a fundamentalist as a separatist. First, last and all the time we are a dyed-in-the-wool Baptist, without frills or furbelows."[61] In a direct rebuke to Norris, the Reverend T. T. Martin protested that to "brand as Modernists, Evolutionists, men who believe in and preach the doctrine of Christ . . . is to traduce and slander brethren, and to injure their work and the work they stand for."[62] "There may be some men dead set on heresy hunting who are upright of character and flawless in their relationship with other people," mused the editor of the *Alabama Baptist*, in 1931, "but unfortunately it has not been this writer's privilege to know such men."[63]

Unabashed by such rebukes and aspersions, the irascible Norris persisted in his savage attacks; and he encouraged his followers to withhold contributions from co-operative denominational enterprises. If Norris reveled in his exclusion from Southern Baptist councils, however, he was not unperturbed by disapprobation from a new quarter. For when he moved toward a final disavowal of the regular Baptist associations, he was repudiated by his long-time mentor and associate, William Bell Riley. Seldom has the binding force of institutional ties been so trenchantly illustrated as in Riley's belated defense of denominational loyalty against the divisive pressures he had himself so much engendered. "The truth is," he concluded in 1931, "that if the fundamentalists of the

[61] Memphis *American Baptist*, June 30, 1926.
[62] *Ibid.*, Apr. 15, 1931.
[63] *Alabama Baptist*, quoted *ibid.*, Aug. 20, 1931.

Baptist denomination are not needed in it now for its sanctification, then they were never needed, and if their lives and labors and influence are not sufficient to accomplish that objective, it is very doubtful if the new organizations being formed by 'Come-Outers' will be any more holy than the one repudiated by them."[64] In 1938 Riley visited ten days with Baptist loyalist clergymen in Dallas and tersely announced that his associations with Norris had been "a serious mistake" and that he had "washed my hands of him forever." He was happy "to be back in the fellowship of men, brethren, in whose course and conduct one can take pleasure." But by this time Norris and his schismatic fundamentalism had ceased to be a serious threat to the Southern Baptist Convention.[65]

It might well be assumed that resurgent conservatism, fratricidal cleavages, and absorption with doctrinal definitions drew southern Protestantism from all earlier paths of social reform endeavor.[66] Yet it was in reform activity that southern Protestants achieved their greatest unity during the 1920's; with equal fervor, conservative, moderate, and liberal churchmen rallied behind prohibition as the great social cause of the ages. Perhaps never has the commitment of American Protestantism to reform through political action been so forthright. The potentialities of the Eighteenth Amendment were exaggerated, and of course the temperance crusade obscured other spheres of concern. But the role assumed by churchmen in promoting prohibition portended a broader, more aggressive interest in social causes generally.

Social spheres other than prohibition were not entirely neglected, however. Church assemblies continued to pro-

[64] William B. Riley, "The Come-Outers," in Fort Worth *Fundamentalist*, Aug. 14, 1931.

[65] The text of Riley's statement was published *ibid.*, Mar. 14, 1938.

[66] Two treatments of Protestant social reform efforts during this period are: Robert Moats Miller, *American Protestantism and Social Issues, 1919–1939* (Chapel Hill, 1958), and Paul A. Carter, *The Decline and Revival of the Social Gospel: Social and Political Liberalism in American Protestant Churches, 1920–1940* (Ithaca, 1954).

nounce on labor conditions, mob violence, and those worldly
injustices which had concerned them in the past. As a rule
such pronouncements were innocuously phrased. A conspicuous exception was an "Appeal to Industrial Leaders of the
South" issued in 1927 by forty-two prominent southern religious leaders. (Among the appellants were three Episcopalian
bishops, five bishops of the Methodist Episcopal Church,
South, and two bishops of the Northern Methodist Episcopal
Church who were assigned to jurisdictions in the South.) The
churchmen decried conditions of labor in southern industry
—low wages, long working hours, use of woman and child
labor, the quartering of industrial workers in company-owned
villages—and called for "employee representation in factory
government" through labor unions or otherwise. "Labor is
human," they proclaimed, "and not a commodity."[67]

Industrial spokesmen reacted with due offense and indig-
nation. The *Manufacturers' Record* charged that "rank Socialism and Bolshevism are coming into play in some ministerial
organizations" and dismissed the allegations as "absolutely
unjustified, untrue, and misleading." Eulogizing industrialists
as "men of high character and of devoted Christian service,"
the *Record* made particular reference to the president of the
National Association of Manufacturers, John E. Edgerton, a
Tennessee textile manufacturer. Edgerton provided a chapel
"where his employees meet each morning for religious service
before entering upon their day's labor. About 90 per cent of
his employees, we have understood, are Christians." Edgerton
himself issued a statement proclaiming that wages "are not
now, never have been and never can be determined by the
necessities of men, nor by moral requirements. Christ himself
did not determine rewards that way, and men cannot do it."
He demanded that emphasis be "put upon work—more work
and better work, instead of upon leisure—more leisure and worse

[67] "An Appeal to Industrial Leaders of the South," in Nashville *Christian
Advocate*, Apr. 7, 1928.

leisure"; he saw an "intimate relationship between leisure and crime." The Charlotte *Observer* defended the "wholesome, moral, healthy and financially happy conditions" which prevailed in company-owned villages, and declared that any breakup of such settlements would be a "shame upon humanity and a crime against God and the Church."[68]

But this controversial appeal did not carry the official endorsement of any church or church agency, and there is no reason to conclude that it reflected a majority viewpoint in any southern denomination. Only five of fourteen bishops of the Southern Methodist Church signed it. The presiding elders and the Commission on Industry of a South Carolina Methodist annual conference regretted that a "little coterie of self-appointed people without authority of the Church . . . should send abroad the impression that their paper represents the judgment and attitude of Southern Methodist Church leaders. . . ." "We have profound appreciation of the great men of South Carolina who pioneered our cotton mill industry," the South Carolinians declared, "and we know them to be statesmen after the order of prophets."[69]

The modernist-fundamentalist controversy reflected wider stirrings in our national life, particularly in the South. For war mobilization and demobilization vastly accelerated change, as did the automobile, the tractor, radios and motion pictures, mass education, the collapse of the rural economy, and a host of other forces. In the decades after World War I, cotton gave way to other tilled crops, to livestock, and to poultry; commercial plantations expanded as family-sized farms diminished; wage hands replaced sharecroppers; chain stores outdated furnishing merchants. A predominantly urban-industrial so-

[68] Baltimore *Manufacturers' Record*, Apr. 21, 28, 1927.
[69] "Reply from South Carolina," in Nashville *Christian Advocate*, Apr. 29, 1927. Liston Pope found in 1942 that "criticism of conditions prevailing in the [textile] industry still elicits from ministers in Gaston County [North Carolina] a recitation of the advantages brought by the mills to the workers and the community." (Liston Pope, *Millhands and Preachers: A Study of Gastonia* [New Haven, 1942], 24.)

ciety was evolving in the South, a society whose norms were increasingly national.[70]

But the transition was not to be accomplished without anguish and contention. Spokesmen of the old order rallied their adherents in churches, schools, and legislatures. Traditionalists in politics and government struggled against poll tax repeal, against municipal autonomy, against lowering racial barriers, against legislative reapportionment. Religious traditionalists continued to stress evangelism and fundamental doctrines; generally they opposed the application of Christian teachings to social conditions, theological training for preachers, and unifications with northern Protestantism. The decade of the 1920's was a particularly critical era in this continuing struggle between the old and the new, between orthodoxy and innovation. Outside church councils, the crisis in religion was reflected in the movement to enact antievolution laws and, less directly, in the presidential campaign of 1928. Many traditionalists sensed that time worked against them.

[70] See Thomas D. Clark, *The Emerging South* (New York, 1961).

4

THE ANTIEVOLUTION CRUSADE

$\mathcal{F}$undamentalist efforts to control education were not without cause and provocation. For per capita expenditure on tax-supported elementary and secondary instruction almost doubled in the United States from 1920 to 1930.[1] With compulsory attendance laws, and with private

[1] US Federal Security Agency, Office of Education, *Statistical Summary of Education, 1947–48* (Washington, 1950), 22, 27, 32, 36.

Furniss, *Fundamentalist Controversy*, though inaccurate in many details, gives the best general treatment of the antievolution movement. Ray Ginger's *Six Days or Forever? Tennessee v. John Thomas Scopes* (Boston, 1958) is a colorful treatment of the Scopes trial, but is not carefully documented; it includes only cursory references to the antievolution crusade. Specific actions to restrict the teaching of evolution in schools are well surveyed in Howard K. Beale, *Are American Teachers Free?* (New York, 1936).

Contemporary accounts published in the *Nation, Current History, New Republic, Independent, Outlook,* and *World's Work* have been especially important in shaping subsequent interpretations. Books heavily relied upon include Arthur Garfield Hays, *Let Freedom Ring* (New York, 1928); Irving Stone, *Clarence Darrow for the Defense* (New York, 1941); William Jennings and Mary B. Bryan, *The Memoirs of William Jennings Bryan* (Phila-

institutions seldom available, conservative parents were impelled increasingly to support and patronize public schools. Forebodings as to the compatibility of religious faith and modern scholarship were heightened by evidences of iconoclasm among students and teachers. Walter Lippmann concluded that "very frequently the difficulty arose because the teacher had failed to teach, and had insisted, sometimes rather provocatively, on announcing strange and unpalatable doctrines which he held to be the truth."[2] A Vanderbilt University philosophy professor lamented that "students coming to the study of science from parents ignorant of science, but having pronounced religious views . . . doubtless have a tendency to underscore what seems to them to be the finalities of science and . . . to manifest extraordinary antipathy to all forms of religion."[3] A respected southern editor was concerned that education commonly led students "from the land of faith to the realm of doubt" and that they emerged often with only "a sneer for the faith of their fathers."[4]

Of course the contradictions between fundamentalism and the theory of evolution were as real and irreconcilable as religious conservatives imagined them to be. This was true even though scientists did not in fact classify man as a descendant of the monkey, and even after the harsh survival-of-the-fittest doctrine was mitigated by the findings of Mendel,

delphia, 1925); Henry Farfield Osborn, *Evolution and Religion in Education: Polemics of the Fundamentalist Controversy of 1922–1926* (New York, 1926); Walter Lippmann, *American Inquisitors: A Commentary on Dayton and Chicago* (New York, 1928); and Henry L. Mencken, *Prejudices: Fifth Series* (New York, 1926). An indispensable state-by-state discussion of the antievolution movement by an ardent opponent is Maynard Shipley, *The War on Modern Science: A Short History of the Fundamentalist Attacks on Evolution and Modernism* (New York, 1927).

[2] Lippmann, *American Inquisitors: A Commentary on Dayton and Chicago*, 94.

[3] Herbert Sanborn, "The Function of Philosophy in Liberal Education," *Peabody Journal of Education*, III (Mar. 1926), 256.

[4] James I. Finney, "The Tennessee Evolution Law," in Nashville *Christian Advocate*, July 31, 1931. Finney was editor of the Nashville *Tennessean*.

de Vries, and others.[5] For it was a cardinal fundamentalist dogma that the Bible must be accepted literally or not at all. If man had evolved by any means from a lower order of life, he obviously was not created by special act as stated in Genesis. And, if Adam and the Garden of Eden were only fictions, so was original sin: "no fall, no real problem of sin; no sin, no need of salvation; no salvation, no Divine Redeemer; and so no Christianity."[6] Fundamentalists campaigned against evolution because the theory was a dire threat to their whole system as they propounded it. Schools were prime targets because they were conspicuous agents of Darwinian contagion.

The crusade for antievolution laws developed without formal general endorsement from any major religious denomination. The 1926 Southern Baptist Convention did unanimously espouse the Genesis account of creation and requested denominational institutions to do likewise.[7] And the Southern Presbyterian General Assembly of 1924 categorically affirmed that "Adam's body was directly fashioned by Almighty God, without any natural parentage of any kind. . . ."[8] But neither convocation made explicit demands on the public schools. On the other hand, the Southern Methodist Educational Association (representing church schools) proclaimed against any interference "with the proper teaching of scientific subjects in American schools and colleges."[9] It seems likely, however, that most southern Protestant clergymen—and many clergymen in rural areas outside the South—came to favor the exclusion of the Darwinian theory from tax-supported institu-

[5] See Robert Scoon, "The Rise and Impact of Evolutionary Ideas," in *Evolutionary Thought in America*, ed. Stow Persons (New York, 1956), 4–42.

[6] *Fundamentalism versus Modernism*, ed. Eldred C. Vanderlaan (New York, 1925), 9. Fundamentalist beliefs are best set forth in *The Fundamentals: A Testimony to the Truth* (12 vols., Chicago, 1909–12).

[7] Southern Baptist Convention, *Annual*, 1926, 18, 98.

[8] Presbyterian Church in the United States, General Assembly, *Minutes*, 1924, 64.

[9] Nashville *Christian Advocate*, Apr. 1, 1927.

tions. Powerful elements of the religious press were similarly inclined, and probably a majority of rank-and-file communicants in the South. Religious denominations often involved themselves on the state and local level. "Modernism and evolution infidelity has crept into our schools and churches just like the loathsome frog creeps into our wells of water," complained the Little Rock *Baptist and Commoner*, "and has defiled our schools and churches just like the frog does the water."[10]

But the antievolution crusade was a special progeny of the interdenominational fundamentalist movement from first to last. Its prime fomenters were leaders in the World's Christian Fundamentals Association, the Bible Crusaders of America, the Antievolution League of America, and other such organizations. William Bell Riley boasted in 1927 that he had won sixteen out of seventeen formal debates on the theory of evolution in cities throughout the nation.[11] "Better wipe out all the schools," exclaimed John Roach Straton, "than undermine belief in the Bible by permitting the teaching of evolution."[12] "If the Bible cannot be taught in tax-supported schools," asked William Jennings Bryan, "why should Christian taxpayers permit the teaching of guesses that make the Bible a lie?"[13] It was these national fundamentalist leaders who took the lead in forcing the issue, in mobilizing public opinion, and in inciting conservative preachers and laymen to act. In the South their calls fell on responsive ears.

The first major drive for a statutory enactment was in Kentucky in 1922. The attempt came after a period of vigorous agitation and after the Baptist State Board of Missions designated a special committee to work for such a law. In the

[10] Quoted in James D. Bernard, "The Baptists," *American Mercury*, VII (Feb. 1926), 139–40.
[11] William Bell Riley, "A Square Deal for Genesis," *Independent*, CXIX (Sept. 12, 1927), 470.
[12] Shipley, *War on Modern Science*, 291.
[13] New York *Times*, Feb. 26, 1922.

forefront was the pastor of the Lexington First Baptist Church, John W. Porter, later cited in *Who's Who* as "the first one in America to bring the evolution question before a state legislature." Porter flaunted a "strength to your arms" endorsement from Bryan when he dramatically announced that "Darwinism would be run out of Kentucky if it took every cent the Baptist people of the Commonwealth had to do it."[14]

Bryan personally presented the issue to a joint meeting of the two houses of the legislature.[15] He also addressed antievolution rallies at Lexington and Danville. Local fundamentalists sponsored newspaper advertisements in a strenuous effort to mobilize opinion. Educators and religious leaders outside the state joined in the discussion. Harvard President Emeritus Charles Eliot refused to believe any legislature would enact such a law. President James R. Angell of Yale believed that the antievolution bills which had been introduced in Kentucky "could not be seriously entertained by any really intelligent person," that they would make the state "the laughing stock of the world," and that they belonged to "the intellectual attitude of the twelfth century." The general secretary of the Federal Council of Churches, Charles F. MacFarland, denounced the measures as "contrary to all the principles on which the American Republic has been founded." "It was marvelous," one observer noted, "how proficient in scientific knowledge the average citizen of Kentucky suddenly became."[16]

Antievolutionists suffered a defeat on February 14 when their bill in the senate was tabled by a nineteen to seventeen

[14] Beatrice Simms, "The Anti-Evolution Conflict in the 1920's," M.A. thesis, University of Kentucky, 1953, includes a scholarly account of the movement in Kentucky. A shorter analysis of the Kentucky campaign is given in Frank L. McVey, *The Gates Open Slowly: A History of Education in Kentucky* (Lexington, 1949), 221–36. *Who's Who in America*, ed. Albert N. Marquis (31 vols., Chicago, 1899–   ), XV (1928–29), 1689.

[15] Kentucky *House Journal*, 1922, 257, 279, *Senate Journal*, 1922, 931.

[16] *Science*, n.s., LV (Feb. 10, 1922), 149–50; Alonzo W. Fortune, "The Kentucky Campaign Against the Teaching of Evolution," in *Journal of Religion*, II (1922), 231–32.

vote. But a more stringent house measure remained to be dealt
with. As drafted, it would prohibit the teaching in tax-supported institutions of "Darwinism, Atheism, Agnosticism, or
the Theory of Evolution in so far as it pertains to the origin
of man"; offending teachers would "on conviction be fined not
less than Fifty ($50.00) dollars nor more than Five Thousand
($5,000) dollars or confined in the County Jail not less than
ten days nor more than twelve months or both fined and im-
prisoned in the discretion of the jury."[17]

Representatives deliberated this harsh measure on March
19, in a tense and crowded chamber. Two guest speakers gave
last-minute appraisals. University of Kentucky President Frank
L. McVey argued for rejection. Approval was urged by a
Frankfort Baptist minister, Noel Gaines, in a lengthy and
impassioned oration. At one point he "ran up and down behind the clerk's desk scattering [zoology textbooks] . . . as
he waved his arms in emphatic gestures. Finally he threw
one of the textbooks to the floor and trampled it under foot."
Spectators laughed and applauded; "Mr. Gaines put William
Jennings Bryan to shame in his denunciations of those who
believe evolution," one reporter marveled.[18]

Voting took place amidst "much scurrying hither and
thither by the advocates and opponents of the bill for the
purpose of finding and dragging in their respective absentees
for the vote"; one legislator frantically phoned his pastor for
advice. Not until the final official tally was completed was
it known that the measure had been defeated by a one-vote
margin, forty-two to forty-one. Fundamentalists were cha-
grined, but they rejoiced more than they sorrowed.[19] "The
movement will sweep the country and we will drive Darwinism
from our schools," Bryan predicted. A Darwinist warned pessi-
mistically that "this is not a time when the scientific world

[17] Kentucky *Senate Journal*, 1922, 1043–46, 1086, *House Journal*, 1922,
1669.
[18] *Science*, n.s., LV (Mar. 24, 1922), 316–18.
[19] *Ibid.*; Kentucky *House Journal*, 1922, 1670.

should regard the situation as a joke, nor merely as a local manifestation. With a 'silver-tongued' apostle, the recrudescence of the old conflict [between science and religion] bids fair to take on the proportions of a general action. . . ."[20]

Kentucky was indeed only an opening skirmish. In succeeding years the crusade gained little momentum in the North and West. Antievolution bills introduced in Maine, New Hampshire, Delaware, West Virginia, Missouri, Minnesota, North Dakota, and California were not seriously considered in most cases; none of these measures won the approval of a single legislative house.[21] But the picture was far different in the South, where legislatures deliberated and redeliberated the issue throughout the 1920's—in North Carolina, in 1925 and 1927; in South Carolina, in 1922, 1927, and 1928; in Georgia, in 1923 and 1925; in Florida, in 1923, 1925, and 1927; in Alabama, in 1923 and 1927; in Mississippi, in 1926; in Louisiana, in 1926; in Texas, in 1923, 1925, and 1929; in Oklahoma, in 1923 and 1927; in Arkansas, in 1927; in Tennessee, in 1923 and 1925; and in Kentucky, in 1922 and 1926.[22] Only Virginia was spared. In a region where piety and religious conservatism ran so deep, evolution was a highly sensitive political issue from the first. A poetic Florida legislator analyzed his dilemma in a verse which he inserted in the house journal:

> To gain my next election
> I know the bill must pass
> So I guess I'll ape the monkey
> By voting like an ass.[23]

Strategy varied from state to state. In some states only a legislative resolution expressing disapproval of Darwinism was

[20] *Science*, n.s., LV (Feb. 17, Mar. 17, 1922), 178, 292.
[21] Maynard Shipley, "Growth of the Anti-Evolution Movement," *Current History and Forum*, XXXII (May, 1930), 330–32, gives a convenient summary of the antievolution bills introduced and the actions taken on them.
[22] *Ibid.*
[23] Florida *House Journal*, 1927, 3002.

sought. Elsewhere textbooks were scrutinized. In at least one state, fundamentalists attempted to withhold public support from institutions "teaching, or permitting to be taught, as a creed to be followed, the cult known as Darwinism."[24] And, in several states besides Kentucky, they sponsored bills with penalty provisions. These bills were often disposed of without fanfare—through adverse committee actions in Tennessee, in 1923, in Kentucky, in 1926, and in North Carolina, in 1927. An Alabama house committee failed to act on an antievolution measure referred to it in 1927. A South Carolina legislative committee held back its report in 1927 until the last hours of the session. And, in 1923, leaders in the Georgia house of representatives refused to steer a committee-approved bill to a final vote.[25]

But where wide attention was aroused, or a vote recorded, such measures usually commanded formidable support in the South. In numerous instances enactment was only narrowly averted. In the South Carolina legislature, in 1922, the senate voted twenty-four to seven for an amendment which would have denied public funds to any school permitting instruction in the theory of evolution; the house refused to concur, however, and the proviso was eliminated in conference committee.[26] In 1923 the Texas house of representatives voted seventy-one to thirty-four to prohibit the teaching in public schools "that man evolved from an ape" (with no penalties provided); the bill won committee approval in the upper house, but was never brought to a final vote. Later that year the Texas lower house resolved eighty-one to nine that Darwinism in public schools was "improper and subversive." But the resolution died in the hands of a senate committee.[27]

[24] South Carolina *Senate Journal*, 1922, 925.
[25] Shipley, "Growth of the Anti-Evolution Movement."
[26] South Carolina *Senate Journal*, 1922, 925, *House Journal*, 1922, 1072.
[27] Texas *House Journal*, 1923, 163, 185, 962, 1164–66, 1459, *House Journal*, 1923 (Third Called Session), 73–74, 83, *Senate Journal*, 1923, 1064–66, 1149, 1509, *Senate Journal*, 1923 (Third Called Session), 40, 340.

Ignoring the pleas of Louisiana State University President Thomas D. Boyd, the Lousiana house of representatives passed an antievolution bill in 1926 by a margin of fifty-two to forty-three. Final enactment was stalled in the senate, however, by a seventeen to fifteen vote for indefinite postponement.[28] In Florida, in 1927, a bill which would have prohibited the teaching in public schools of atheism, infidelity, or any theory denying "the divine creation of man" (and which prescribed penalties in fines up to $100) was approved sixty-seven to twenty-four in the house of representatives; but the senate education committee refused to recommend it, and a special move to force final action was defeated nineteen to fifteen.[29] And, in Arkansas that same year, the lower house voted fifty to forty-seven for an antievolution proposal after a "desperate fight" during which the bill was first rejected; the senate tabled the measure, however, and later voted seventeen to fourteen against further consideration.[30]

But all such fundamentalist efforts did not end in frustration. In five southern states—Oklahoma, Florida, Tennessee, Mississippi, and Arkansas—antievolution measures won final approval. The first enactment came in Oklahoma, in 1923, as an amendment to a free textbook bill. Although the Baptist General Session of Oklahoma had memorialized the legislature "regarding the matter of the teaching of evolution in our public school system," the introduction of the anti-evolution amendment came without forewarning. Indeed the move "struck the house like a thunderclap" and was construed by free textbook proponents as a strategem to "load down and kill" the parent legislation.[31] The amendment stipulated that

[28] Louisiana *House Journal*, 1926, 167, 190, 575, 700, 762–63, *Senate Journal*, 1926, 597.

[29] Florida *House Journal*, 1927, 137, 773–74, 2331–35, 2773, 2998–3002, *Senate Journal*, 1927, 2412, 2416, 3069.

[30] Arkansas *House Journal*, 1927, 323–25, *Senate Journal*, 1927, 317, 351.

[31] Oklahoma City *Daily Oklahoman*, Feb. 22, 1923. R. Halliburton, Jr., "The Nation's First Anti-Darwin Law," *Southwestern Social Science Quar-*

"no copyright shall be purchased, nor text book adopted that teaches the 'materialistic Conception of History' (i.e.) The Darwinian Theory of Creation vs. the Bible Account of Creation."[32] Shouts of "lie" and threats of physical violence were part of the spirited debate that ensued. House opponents derided the amendment as a "step toward the dark ages" and hinted that it was instigated by "book interests." But the anti-Darwinians stood their ground. "I promised my people at home that if I had a chance to down this hellish Darwin here that I would do it," one legislator exclaimed, ". . . I am for this amendment and will strike this infernal thing while I can!" When the proposal won tentative thirty-eight to thirty-three approval in the committee of the whole, the majority floor leader withdrew his objections. Afterward only one representative recorded his opposition. Thus amended, the textbook bill passed the house by vote of eighty-seven to two.[33]

The proposal was much discussed during the interval between the house action on February 21 and final senate action on March 22. The Oklahoma City *Times* strongly condemned it.[34] The Reverend Frank Hampton Fox, pastor of Park Congregational Church in Oklahoma City, feigned surprise that the representatives "did not exercise their august powers to bring a few of the teachers of science from the state institutions before them, to place them in electrically charged chairs and couches, and then to re-enact some of the minor horrors at least of the old Roman inquisition to get them to recant what they have said and written." An official at Methodist-sponsored Oklahoma City College confirmed that the theory of evolution was taught there and "accepted by all people

terly, XLI (Sept., 1960), 123–35, is a competent study of the Oklahoma enactment.
   [32] Oklahoma *Laws*, 1923, 296.
   [33] Oklahoma City *Daily Oklahoman*, Feb. 22, 1923.
   [34] Oklahoma City *Times*, Feb. 23, 1923.

who think."[35] Proponents of the amendment were equally articulate. The clerk of the state supreme court proclaimed that "there is a fundamental difference between letting a person think as he pleases and in using time and service which the state pays for and which belongs to the state in teaching the children of others theories that are not Biblical. . . ."[36] The Oklahoma City superintendent of public schools opined that "the state should keep everything out of text books that would tend to destroy faith in God." And the state Baptist Sunday School Convention unanimously adopted a resolution congratulating the house of representatives for its action. The state board of education insisted that none of its previous textbook adoptions propounded the Darwinian theory.[37]

Thus pressured and advised, the senate incorporated the antievolution amendment into its version of the textbook bill; and the amendment remained in the law as finally enacted. "But the processes of evolution will continue, even though instruction in such science is denied," the Oklahoma City *Times* editorialized. "In time they may produce a legislature broader-minded than the gentlemen who tried witches down Salem way."[38]

Two months later the Florida legislature adopted a resolution proclaiming its "sense" that it was "improper and subversive to the best interest of the people of this State" for public school teachers to teach "atheism, or agnosticism, or to teach as true Darwinism, or any other hypothesis that links man in blood relationship to other forms of life."[39] Neither the Florida nor Oklahoma action was of any great significance, however. The Florida legislature merely recorded its opinion. The Oklahoma enactment pertained only to text-

[35] *Ibid.*, Feb. 22, 26, 1923.
[36] Oklahoma City *Daily Oklahoman*, Mar. 4, 1923.
[37] Oklahoma City *Times*, Feb. 22, 23, 1923. The Tulsa superintendent of schools criticized the amendment. Halliburton, "The Nation's First Anti-Darwin Law," 127.
[38] Oklahoma City *Times*, Mar. 22, 1923.
[39] Florida *Acts, 1923*, 50.

books used through the eighth grade, and it expired two years later when the parent textbook legislation was repealed.[40]

And so it was in Tennessee, in 1925, that the antievolutionists gained their first substantial legislative victory. A similar attempt in 1923 had failed after adverse committee actions in both houses.[41] But religious conservatives continued their efforts. Early in 1924 William Jennings Bryan addressed a mammoth fundamentalist rally in Nashville from a platform on which the Democratic governor, a Republican ex-governor, and other prominent Tennesseans were seated. With his usual eloquence, the Commoner flayed Darwinism and exhorted believers in Biblical inerrancy to stand fast; listeners cheered, shouted, and reacted otherwise like his "old-time political gatherings."[42] When legislators convened a year later, copies of Bryan's speech were distributed among them.[43] On January 21, 1925, Macon County Representative John Washington Butler introduced House Bill 185, to forbid teaching in public schools "any theory that denies the story of the Divine Creation of man as taught in the Bible, and to teach instead that man has descended from a lower order of animals"; the bill prescribed a fine of from $100 to $500 for offending teachers.[44] Final house approval came only six days later, seventy-one to five. Church of Christ and Baptist groups conspicuously supported the bill; the Nashville Baptist Pastors

---

[40] Oklahoma *Laws*, 1925, 10. A $950,000 appropriation had proven insufficient to finance textbook purchases during the biennium 1923–25. A special referendum on the free textbook law in 1926 failed to reverse the action of the 1925 legislature. But discussion of the antievolution proviso was quite incidental in the debate over the statute as a whole.

[41] Tennessee *House Journal*, 1923, 666, 719, 720, *Senate Journal*, 1923, 599, 605, 668. The enactment of the Tennessee law is treated in Kenneth K. Bailey, "The Enactment of Tennessee's Antievolution Law," *Journal of Southern History*, XVI (Nov. 1950), 472–90.

[42] Nashville *Banner*, Feb. 24, 1924; *Nashville Tennessean*, Feb. 25, 1924.

[43] Interview with W. B. Marr, Nashville, Tennessee, June, 11, 1948. See William Jennings and Mary B. Bryan, *Memoirs of William Jennings Bryan*, 481.

[44] Tennessee *Public Acts*, 1925, 50–51.

Council claimed its endorsement spoke for "ten thousand laymen of twenty local churches."[45]

Protests were nonavailing. The house adopted an extraordinary resolution belittling a Columbia, Tennessee, Methodist minister's criticisms as "unfair, unchristianlike and unpatriotic."[46] Nor was the senate swayed by an opposing petition signed by fourteen prominent Nashville clergymen. Following a personal appeal for passage by Speaker Lew D. Hill (a member of the Church of Christ), senators voted twenty-four to six for the measure. Pleas for a gubernatorial veto—one from a delegation headed by Bruce R. Payne, president of George Peabody College for Teachers—were also fruitless.[47] On March 23, Governor Austin Peay signed the bill into law, although he explained in a special message that he regarded it as a mere "protest against an irreligious tendency" and not as a statute to be enforced.[48] The governor's efforts to depreciate the law's significance did not succeed. The New York *Times* gave the enactment front-page coverage. Even before the Scopes litigation, Tennessee's "monkey law" became known throughout the nation.[49]

Less celebrated but equally drastic were laws passed in Mississippi and Arkansas after the bizarre Scopes trial. The 1926 Mississippi law carried a penalty provision similar to that of the Tennessee act and pertained to textbook adoptions as well as to the teaching of evolution. It was passed by the legislature

[45] Tennessee *House Journal*, 1925, 210; Nashville *Tennessean*, Mar. 25, 1925; Nashville *Evening Tennessean*, Mar. 23, 1925.

[46] Tennessee *House Journal*, 1925, 358.

[47] Tennessee *Senate Journal*, 1925, 517; Nashville *Tennessean*, Mar. 14, 1925; Nashville *Banner*, Mar. 13, 1925. No major Tennessee newspaper advocated the enactment of the Butler bill; the Memphis *Commercial Appeal* (Feb. 8, 1925) and the Chattanooga *Daily Times* (Feb 7, 1925), published editorials opposing it.

[48] Tennessee *House Journal*, 1925, 741–45.

[49] New York *Times*, Mar. 24, 1925. Ray Ginger makes the incredible assertion that officials of the American Civil Liberties Union, in New York, who initiated the Scopes litigation, learned of the law from a "three inch item in a Tennessee newspaper" called to their attention by an alert secretary. Ginger, *Six Days or Forever?*, 18.

and signed by the governor despite adverse committee actions in both houses, opposition in the state press, and a warning from University of Mississippi Chancellor Alfred Hume that teachers would be compelled "to evade, disregard, or openly violate the law, or . . . be guilty of intellectual dishonesty."[50] A local Baptist association had petitioned the legislature to prevent "this snake in the grass [evolution] from injecting its poison into the minds and hearts of the school-children of this State"; but observers stressed the role of a "powerful lobby of the Bible Crusaders" who had "been there several weeks organizing the church forces in behalf of the bill."[51] The Reverend Thomas T. Martin, serving as a Bible Crusader lobbyist, addressed the house of representatives. He spoke in behalf of a committee minority report which alleged that "Infidels, Agnostics, Modernists and all the mongrel forces that tend to destroy virtue . . . are using our educational institutions as propaganda bureaus."[52] "Shall the legislature of Mississippi barter the faith of the children of Mississippi in God's word and in the Savior for the fulsome praise of a paganized press?" Martin asked.[53] During a heated debate, representatives rejected a farcical amendment which would have prescribed a penalty of "death by burning at stake, it being the spirit of this bill to restore the Spanish inquisition." When final action came in the lower house, seventy-six legislators voted for the bill, thirty-two against. The senate concurred twenty-nine to sixteen, after an emotional three-hour debate before crowded galleries. Governor Henry L. Whitfield then added his approval.[54]

Last of the antievolution statutes to be enacted was the one which became law in Arkansas in 1928. Only in this in-

[50] "Banishing Evolution from the South," *Literary Digest,* XXCIX, Apr. 3, 1926, 30; Shipley, *War on Modern Science,* 71–72.

[51] *Ibid.;* Memphis *Commercial Appeal,* Feb. 5, 9, 24, 25, 1926.

[52] Mississippi *House Journal,* 1926, 330.

[53] Shipley, *War on Modern Science,* 65.

[54] Mississippi *House Journal,* 1926, 559–666, *Senate Journal,* 1926, 929, *Laws,* 1926, 435; Memphis *Commercial Appeal,* Feb. 10, 25, 1926.

stance was the question carried directly to the electorate. When the 1927 legislature failed to pass an antievolution law, the Reverend Ben M. Bogard (a Little Rock Landmark Baptist) and others drafted a similar measure into an initiative petition. They proposed to outlaw the teaching of Darwinism in public schools and to prohibit use of textbooks in which the theory was propounded; offenders would be fined up to $500.[55] The petition with the required signatures was filed with the secretary of state on June 6, 1928, thus invoking a referendum that fall. Public excitement quickened when Charles Smith, president of the American Association for the Advancement of Atheism, accepted Bogard's challenge to debate. Both men were severely criticized for inflammatory conduct. Bogard sued the El Dorado *Daily News* for holding "this plaintiff up before the public as a fanatic"; Smith was arrested in Little Rock for distributing literature "calculated to disturb the peace." Even the conservative Memphis *Commercial Appeal* editorialized that "maybe there will be an election in which the voters of varying degrees of intellectual attainments will be asked to decide upon the Einstein theory of relativity or the new idea of atom construction and energy."[56] But ridicule did not dissuade Arkansas voters. By a majority of 108,991 to 63,406 they voted the initiative petition into law. State Superintendent of Instruction Joseph P. Womack at first construed the statute to exclude the *Encyclopaedia Britannica*, the *World Book Encyclopedia*, and *Webster's International Dictionary* from public school libraries. The dean of the state medical school lamented that compliance would undermine medical instruction.[57]

Yet, notwithstanding such forebodings, and the ballyhoo of the Scopes trial, the antievolution statutes did not become

[55] Arkansas *Laws, 1929*, II, 1518–19.
[56] *Nation*, CXXVII (Nov. 21, 1928), 533; Memphis *Commercial Appeal*, Nov. 9, 1928.
[57] Memphis *Commercial Appeal*, Nov. 14, 1928.

major instruments of oppression. Bryan had urged in the first place that no penalty provisions be incorporated in the Tennessee law.[58] Governor Peay emphasized when he signed the measure that he did not expect it to be enforced.[59] Most law enforcement officers outside Dayton seemed to regret the prosecution of Scopes. And the Tennessee Supreme Court, in upholding the constitutionality of the Butler Act, requested that the litigation pending under it be *nol-prossed*.[60] There were no further prosecutions under the Tennessee law.

The Mississippi and Arkansas enactments were also to become dead letters. The Mississippi attorney general refused to clarify his state's antievolution statute. "Inasmuch as it is assumed that the teachers . . . are supposed to be intelligent men and women and are supposed to be good men and women," he wrote an inquiring professor, ". . . I feel that it would be presumptuous on my part in this opinion to give out any gratuitous statements . . . that would in any way enlighten you as to how you are to teach school, and merely content myself with the belief that you will in the future as in the past teach your pupils to look through nature up to nature's god. . . ."[61] The Tennessee, Mississippi, and Arkansas laws remain on the statute books, but are not actively enforced.

Of greater consequence than the antievolution statutes were actions by officials controlling textbook adoptions. In 1924 the North Carolina state board of education announced

---

[58] See Bryan's letter to Senator John A. Shelton, in William Jennings and Mary B. Bryan, *Memoirs of William Jennings Bryan*, 482.

[59] "Nobody believes that it is going to be an active statute." (Tennessee *House Journal*, 1925, 741–45.)

[60] 154 Tennessee 121. The court overruled the judgment against Scopes on a technicality; his fine had been erroneously assessed by the presiding judge rather than by the jury.

[61] The letter was published in the Nashville *Christian Advocate*, Apr. 1, 1927. For more recent replies by state officials to queries about the antievolution laws, see Raymond H. Robison, "The Scopes Trial: A Case Study in Fundamentalism," M.A. thesis, Pennsylvania State College, 1950, 117.

it would not adopt any biology text which contradicted the Genesis account of creation.[62] The Tennessee textbook commission hurriedly changed its high school biology adoption, in June 1925, after Scopes was indicted for teaching from the textbook then prescribed.[63] That same year the Texas state textbook commission directed publishers to remove references to Darwinism from texts prior to delivery for use in Texas public schools.[64] And, heeding the petition of a committee of the state Baptist convention, in 1926, the Louisiana state superintendent of education requested publishers to delete offensive passages from high school biology textbooks. Meanwhile, he directed secondary teachers to omit specified pages in their coverage.[65] At least some authors and publishers were co-operative. One publisher agreed to omit three chapters from a biology text used in Texas. Another told of textual alterations in a health book at the behest of a state commission. One publishing house boasted that its texts had been "tactfully" written so as not to offend. "Mutilated and garbled versions of books used elsewhere cannot be a source of satisfaction to anyone," complained the New York *Times*, "and one might expect it to be a cause of severe heartsearchings on the part of both publishers and authors."[66]

Nor did the religious conservatives always confine their scrutiny of textbooks to biological and scientific treatises. Hence in 1943 the Kentucky General Association of Baptists proclaimed that the Rugg Social Science Series was unfit for use in public schools; this state convocation also exhorted each local Baptist association to designate a committee "to look into the public school text books used in its locality and to work with the State Text-book Committee of Kentucky

---

[62] New York *Times*, Jan. 24, 1924.

[63] Nashville *Banner*, June 10, 11, 1925.

[64] New York *Times*, Oct. 17, 1925; Memphis *Commercial Appeal*, Feb. 10, 1926.

[65] Louisiana State Baptist Convention, *Annual*, 1926 (n.p., n.d.), 18, 20, 21.

[66] New York *Times*, July 13, 14, 1926.

Baptists." Special vigilance was asked against "anti-Christian or un-American propaganda."[67]

Control of teacher recruitment and tenure was even more vital. Scopes' replacement was Raleigh E. Valentine Reece, brother of B. Carroll Reece. The new appointee was a graduate of Baptist-operated Carson-Newman College and did not "credit the theory that man descended from a lower order of animals."[68] Had this not been the case, his future at Dayton would have been insecure; the school superindentent had earlier promised that "under no circumstances will I ever recommend any person who is not a fundamentalist."[69] Also in Tennessee, the Carroll County board of education resolved in the summer of 1925 not to hire any teacher who believed in the evolutionary theory, or who denied the divinity of Christ; the Maury County board announced a similar policy.[70] Although few boards were so explicit, such criteria no doubt weighed heavily with school trustees throughout the South (and in some areas outside the South). "The teacher who fails to recognize his or her obligation to our youth, our homes, our churches, will soon be discovered by the people of the community as a liability, rather than an asset, and will soon be looking for a new place," the Lubbock First Baptist Church served notice.[71] Howard K. Beale surmised in 1941 that more than one out of three American teachers were "afraid to express acceptance of the theory of evolution, even if they make no effort to persuade their pupils."[72] In 1963 two Memphis State University student teachers were reprimanded by a high school principal for discussing the theory of evolution before a biology class. The young teachers heeded the principal's counsel and made no effort to force another court

[67] Louisville *Western Recorder*, Sept. 21, 1944.
[68] New York *Times*, Aug. 17, 1925.
[69] Nashville *Banner*, June 17, 1925.
[70] *Ibid.*, May 28, 1925; Nashville *Tennessean*, June 5, 1925.
[71] Lubbock *First Baptist*, Sept. 8, 1933.
[72] Howard K. Beale, *A History of Freedom of Teaching in American Schools* (New York, 1941), 241.

test of the 1925 law. "We could not continue this without jeopardizing the Memphis State student teachers program," one of them declared.[73] The incident brought sorrowful comments from John Thomas Scopes, now in semiretirement at Shreveport, Louisiana. He expressed doubt that the Dayton litigation accomplished much toward bringing the theory of evolution and modern science into public schools. "I think the case was lost in 1925. We fought a good battle but we didn't win very much. I would hope it would be different today, but I don't really know."[74]

More than any episode of this century, the antievolution crusade dramatized the conservative religious temper of the South and popularized the Bible Belt stereotype. It did more than this, however. For nonsouthern ridicule solidified southerners and activated defensive psychological mechanisms. This was especially evident at the time of the Scopes trial. "There need be no concern [at] what scoffers of the world may say," Governor Peay declared; "I have a profound contempt for those who are throwing slurs at Tennessee."[75] The Nashville *Tennessean* decried "unfounded criticism and misrepresentation," assured northern critics its readers were unabashed by their "spasms" over Scopes' prosecution, and boasted that the forbears of the people of Tennessee were fighting for freedom of thought, speech, and religion "while the ancestors of the present population of New York City were dimly hearing of America as a far off land."[76] The Oklahoma Society of Tennesseans deprecated "beyond words the untruthful and slanderous verbal pictures drawn of residents of Dayton and vicinity."[77] A self-styled "Yokel of Rhea County," Tennessee, opined that Henry L. Mencken—one of Dayton's most caustic critics—had " 'evolved' from . . . the

[73] Birmingham *News*, Apr. 7, 1963.
[74] Nashville *Tennessean*, Apr. 6, 1963.
[75] Nashville *Banner*, June 26, 1925.
[76] Nashville *Tennessean*, June 2, 1925.
[77] Memphis *Commercial Appeal*, July 16, 1925.

skunk and the tumblebug (with apologies to both) as he surely exhibits the more offensive characteristics of both to a remarkable degree."[78] And John E. Edgerton warned that the "walking delegates of agnosticism, atheism, communism, and bolshevism" were converging on Dayton.[79]

In admonishing their traducers, southerners turned often to a defense and a eulogy of the southern way of life. "Our critics have made sport of us largely because Tennessee has dared to hold to its own personality and has refused to cast itself in a melting pot of new ideals and ambitions," complained the Chattanooga *News*, then edited by George Fort Milton.[80] Bishop Warren A. Candler rejoiced with the *Manufacturer's Record* that the Scopes trial was "one of the South's supremest advertisements" in publicizing a region where religion "pure and undefiled still holds sway." Candler quoted approvingly the *Record*'s contrast of the piety of the South with the "agnosticism and atheism so prevalent throughout the North and West."[81]

---

[78] Chattanooga *News*, July 28, 1925.
[79] Nashville *Banner*, June 29, 1925.
[80] Chattanooga *News*, July 23, 1925.
[81] Warren A. Candler, "Liberalism Proposing to Liberate the South," in Nashville *Christian Advocate*, Sept. 18, 1925.

5

THE CAMPAIGN OF 1928

$\mathcal{F}$ew episodes are more vital to a study of southern Protestantism than the presidential campaign of 1928. Emphasizing prohibition and the menace of a Catholic president, Protestant clergymen embarked on a crusade to carry the South for Hoover. "Vote as you pray," one advertisement urged.[1] Not since the turbulent Populist uprisings

[1] Memphis *Commercial Appeal*, Nov. 4, 1928. Churches and clergymen participated conspicuously in the campaign throughout the nation, but their role was not usually a predominant one except in the South. In most nonsouthern areas Hoover's campaign was in the hands of regular party leaders. Nor did prohibition and Catholicism dominate the debate so much nationally as they did in the South.

Edmund A. Moore's monograph corroborates the early conclusion of Roy V. Peel and Thomas C. Donnelly that economic prosperity afforded the Republicans their greatest advantage in the nation as a whole. In an able summary, Richard Hofstadter points to Hoover's enormous personal popularity, to "the hopeless condition of the Democratic Party when Smith took it over," and to Smith's inability to find a "good issue." Of course, prohibition was an issue in all parts of the country, as was Smith's religious faith. (Edmund A. Moore, *A Catholic Runs for President: The Campaign of 1928*

92

in the 1890's was the region so rent by political agitation. Fighting broke out between loyalist and defecting factions in the Texas State Democratic Convention, producing what was described as the "wildest scenes that ever marked a Democratic meeting" in that state; "many of the state's most prominent political leaders swung their fists in a free-for-all," "eyes were blackened and noses bled." Violence and threats of violence often interrupted political rallies. "Let those who preach tolerance to us practice tolerance themselves," pleaded Southern Methodist University President Charles C. Selecman; "rotten eggs thrown at defenders of Prohibition are a poor show of tolerance." A Baptist minister presiding at a Jackson, Mississippi, gathering begged that "if eggs are to be thrown, or if bullets are to be fired," they be directed at him rather than at the main speaker. Election-day fracases in Kentucky were blamed for at least six deaths.[2] It was an ordeal of violence and retaliation, of invective and counterinvective.

And it was an ordeal in which the Southern Baptist and Methodist denominations played a central role. For it is one thing when a preacher acts politically without special reference to the actions of other clergymen; it is quite another when ecclesiastical leaders initiate and direct a campaign for a specific candidate, in concert with the denominational press,

[New York, 1956], 195; Roy V. Peel and Thomas C. Donnelly, *The Campaign of 1928: An Analysis* [New York, 1931], 71; Richard Hofstadter, "Could a Protestant Have Beaten Hoover in 1928?" *The Reporter*, Mar. 17, 1960, 30–31. See also Herbert Hoover, *The Memoirs of Herbert Hoover* [3 vols., New York, 1951–52], II, 201; Oscar Handlin, *Al Smith and His America* [Boston, 1958]; Emily Smith Warner, *The Happy Warrior: A Biography of My Father, Alfred E. Smith* [Garden City, 1956]; Alfred E. Smith, *Up to Now* [New York, 1929]; and Ruth C. Silva, *Rum, Religion and Votes: 1928 Re-Examined* [University Park, Pa., 1962].)

[2] El Paso *Times*, Sept. 12, Oct. 24, 1928; Shreveport *Journal*, Nov. 1, 1928; Memphis *Commercial Appeal*, Oct. 4, 6, 9, 1928; New Orleans *Times-Picayune*, Sept. 22, Nov. 1, 8, 1928. For a penetrating analysis of the election in the South, see V. O. Key, Jr., *Southern Politics in State and Nation* (New York, 1950). See also Francis B. Simkins, *A History of the South* (New York, 1958), 560; John Samuel Ezell, *The South Since 1865* (New York, 1963), 412; Samuel Lubell, *The Future of American Politics* (Garden City, 1956), 120–25.

and in conformity with denominational policy pronouncements. The latter was the pattern in the South in 1928. Seldom
if ever have major religious groups in America become so
intimately involved in a partisan debate.

Of course the crusade developed out of tendencies previously well defined. In the period before World War I southern Protestantism had stressed the application of Christian
ideals to the social order and the duty of churches to strive
for social betterment. But social reform commitments usually
aroused dissension, and in the 1920's they became a central
issue in the critically divisive modernist-fundamentalist controversy. Only on legal prohibition could virtually all Protestant
clergymen unite in espousing a reform cause. Hence, in emphasizing this, clerical leaders accommodated reform commitments
to the needs of denominational harmony.[3] "The fact is daily becoming more evident," declared the Southern Methodist
General Conference of 1922, "that the adoption of Prohibition by the United States was the most important, far-reaching enactment ever put upon the Statute Books of any nation."
In a report in 1926 the Southern Methodist Commission on
Temperance and Social Service conceded that "the Commission, while it has endeavored to strike a clear note on all the
applications of the gospel of Jesus to the entire social order,
has, somewhat through force of circumstances, majored on
the question of prohibition and law enforcement."[4] The
Southern Baptist Convention had rationalized a similar
emphasis earlier:

Hand in hand with the liquor traffic goes everything evil.
Abolish that and to a large extent you abolish the gambling den
and the den of vice, for these are found almost invariably in connection with the saloon. You abolish also many of the evils of the

[3] Paul Carter discusses the tendency among clergymen *"to make Prohibition
a surrogate for the Social Gospel."* Carter, *Decline and Revival of the Social
Gospel,* 42.
[4] Methodist Episcopal Church, South, General Conference, *Journal,* 1922,
241; *Journal,* 1926, 384.

sweat shop, if not the sweat shop itself. You abolish child labor, for then the father will be able to earn a living for the family without forcing his children to labor to support themselves and him. You go far toward abolishing the crowded tenement, for with the father as the wage-earner each family will be able to have its own little home.[5]

"Are the physical, economical, domestic and moral conditions better in the United States since the adoption of the prohibition law or are they worse?" asked the Amite River (Louisiana) Baptist Association, in 1928. The association rejoiced that they were better:

Careful investigations by men and women of standing and reputation prove that labor has been enriched. Business enlarged, public savings and capital resources vastly increased. Social conditions improved, public health benefited and morality advanced, home conditions are better on food and clothing, comforts and conveniences. There has been a striking increase of personal ownership of homes and in recreation, amusements and school opportunities.[6]

To this recital of blessings which prohibition had wrought the enhancement of denominational harmony might well have been added. For prohibition served to calm and moderate internal dissensions and to draw warring factions into a common cause and purpose.

Southern Baptists and Methodists officially made known their attitude toward Smith long before he won the Democratic nomination. The previous Southern Methodist General Conference, in 1926, condemned all nonprohibition candidates for public office, "from revenue agent to President."[7] The following year four Southern Methodist bishops issued statements specifically denouncing the New York governor; "the attitude of Governor Smith on the issue of national

[5] Southern Baptist Convention, *Annual, 1916* (Atlanta, n.d.), 72.

[6] Amite River (Louisiana) Baptist Association, *Minutes, 1928* (n.p., n.d.), 7.

[7] Methodist Episcopal Church, South, General Conference, *Journal, 1926,* 292.

prohibition makes his candidacy impossible of my support and thousands of whom I can confidently speak," one of the statements declared.[8] A convention of Southern Methodist educators formally proclaimed that "the nomination of Al Smith would be unfortunate and, in our opinion, would not enlist the support of the educational leaders of the South."[9] On the eve of the Democratic Convention the Southern Methodist Board of Missions (largest and most representative board of the church) issued an extraordinary statement opposing all candidates not "positively and openly" committed to prohibition.[10] Having warned in 1924 that "no political party can ride to the White House on a beer keg," the Southern Baptist Convention resolved in 1927 that "no man who is a friend of the outlawed and persistently lawless liquor traffic, or who stands for the nullification of the Constitution and the laws of the United States should receive our support."[11] Even more directly, the convention in 1928 observed that one "prominently mentioned" for the Presidential nomination "is not only a staunch friend of the liquor traffic but a man who by all the power at his command has sought to nullify the Constitution." Then, having thus observed, the convention took this unprecedented action:

Resolved, "that by the adoption of this report we enter into a sacred convenant and solemn pledge that we will support for the office of President, or for any other office, only such men as stand for our present order of prohibition, for the faithful and efficient

[8] Bishops Horace M. Du Bose, John M. Moore, H. A. Boaz, and James M. Cannon, Jr.; the quotation is from the Du Bose statement. All mentioned Smith's Catholicism as a disqualification except Bishop Boaz. Nashville *Christian Advocate*, May 6, 1927.

[9] Jackson *Baptist Record*, Feb. 23, 1928. The resolution was that of the Southern Methodist Educational Association.

[10] *Bishop Cannon's Own Story*, ed. Richard L. Watson, Jr., (Durham, 1955), 406, 409–11.

[11] Southern Baptist Convention, *Annual, 1924*, 116; *Annual, 1927* (Nashville, n.d.), 118.

enforcement of all law, and for the maintenance and support of
the Constitution of the United States in all its parts and with all
its amendments," and that we record our fixed determination to
oppose actively the nomination or the election of any candidate
of the opposite type no matter by what party put forward nor on
what party platform they may stand.[12]

Never before had the two largest bodies of southern Protestantism committed themselves in such manner in a partisan
political campaign.

More than anyone else, it was the chairmen of the Southern
Baptist and Methodist temperance and social service commissions—the Reverend Arthur J. Barton and Bishop James
M. Cannon, Jr.—who steered their denominations into the
thick of the fight. Following Smith's nomination, the two
issued a call for a conference of southerners to organize for

[12] Southern Baptist Convention, *Annual,* 1928 (n.p., n.d.), 88. The pronouncement made no reference to Smith's religious faith. This was also true
of the 1926 pronouncement of the General Conference of the Methodist
Episcopal Church, South, and generally true of the anti-Smith pronouncements of Methodist annual conferences, and those of Baptist district and
state conventions and associations.

On the other hand, on the eve of the 1960 campaign the Southern Baptist
Convention adopted a resolution suggesting that Catholic beliefs on church-
state relationships disqualified one of that faith from holding high public
office; at least eight state Southern Baptist conventions made similar pronouncements in 1960. The Methodist Church and its annual conferences in
the South eschewed such anti-Kennedy pronouncements. The prominent involvement of southern Churches of Christ in the 1960 campaign had little precedent in 1928. Churches of Christ have no intercongregational agencies or
convocations, and they were numerically weak in 1928; the Nashville *Gospel
Advocate,* privately owned Church of Christ paper, did not align itself with
the anti-Smith crusade. Baton Rouge *State Times,* May 19, 1960; Baton
Rouge *Morning Advocate,* May 21, 1960; "Campaign: Religion Becomes an
Open Issue," in *U. S. News and World Report,* Sept. 12, 1960, 94; Nashville *Gospel Advocate,* 1928, *passim.*

Southern Presbyterians did not become involved in the 1928 campaign
as a denomination, as the Southern Baptists and Methodists did. The Southern
Presbyterian General Assembly had long advocated legal prohibition, and in
principle the election of prohibitionist public officials. However, the assembly
pointedly avoided political commitments in 1928, and the Southern Presbyterian press refrained from openly endorsing Hoover.

his defeat. Only in this manner, they declared, could the "ideals and unity of Southern Democracy" be preserved.[13] On July 18 approximately two hundred invited laymen and preachers assembled in Asheville, North Carolina, organized themselves into a Conference of anti-Smith Democrats, and, on nomination of Bishop Cannon, unanimously elected Barton permanent chairman. Moving along "under the directing hand of Dr. Barton," the conference completed its deliberations and adjourned the following day. Its major work was a "Declaration of Principles and Purpose," which made no reference to Smith's religion, but scathingly denounced his stand on prohibition, his conduct as Governor of New York, and his nomination "in defiance of the known wishes of the Democracy of the South." A full-scale campaign to elect Republican-pledged electors was planned. The effort would be directed by an anti-Smith Democratic executive committee comprised of two representatives from each southern state, and a nine-member advisory committee to include Cannon and Barton.[14]

The Southern Methodist and Southern Baptist press—denominationally owned and controlled with only a few exceptions—enthusiastically supported the movement. In an editorial entitled "How Would Jesus Vote?" the *Oklahoma Methodist* assured loyalist-minded Democrats "He would belong to no parties," and that "He would vote against His brother if His brother were wrong."[15] The Arkansas

[13] Asheville *Citizen,* June 30, 1928; Nashville *Christian Advocate,* July 13, 1928. The Southern Methodist Temperance and Social Service Commission was reconstituted as a "Board" in 1926.

[14] Asheville *Citizen,* July 19, 20, 1928. The "Declaration of Principles and Purpose" is given in Watson, *Bishop Cannon's Own Story,* 422–27.

For treatments of the 1928 campaign in two southern states, see Leslie M. Gower, "The Election of 1928 in Tennessee," M.A. thesis, Vanderbilt University, 1959, and Nevin E. Neal, "The Smith-Robinson Arkansas Campaign of 1928," in *Arkansas Historical Quarterly,* XIX (1960), 3–11. Joe B. Frantz gives a brief but penetrating analysis in "A Historian Looks Back to '28," in Austin *Texas Observer,* Sept. 30, 1960.

[15] Quoted in Nashville *Christian Advocate,* July 20, 1928. The Nashville

Baptist Advance reasoned that "in the present presidential campaign we can afford to be called traitors to the party . . . rather than actual traitors to Christ and the cause of righteousness."[16] "The Baptist press is almost a unit in its informed and fearless reaction to the challenge of a soaking wet presidential candidate," declared the Kentucky *Western Recorder*.[17] A Methodist preacher rejoiced that eighteen out of twenty papers published under the auspices of the Southern Baptist and Methodist denominations "are openly and boldly for decency, morality and good government in this crisis," and that "the other two are certainly not supporting Al Smith."[18]

Of course the movement attracted powerful support from non-Baptist and non-Methodist elements, including many clergymen of other communions. No organization promoted the cause more fervently than the Anti-Saloon League. Yet the league was a creature of evangelical Protestantism: Barton was chairman, and Bishop Cannon a member, of its national executive committee; most of its state superintendents were clergymen; its program was normally channeled through local congregations.[19] A few well-known politicians gave their sup-

---

Christian Advocate was the general weekly organ of the Methodist Episcopal Church, South, published under the auspices of the General Conference. State Methodist papers were sponsored by annual conferences.

[16] Little Rock *Baptist Advance*, Aug. 2, 1928. This paper was an organ of the state convention. With only a few exceptions, Baptist papers in the South had been brought under the control of state conventions in the early 1920's. See Patrick Henry Hill, "The Ethical Emphases of the Baptist Editors in the Southeastern Region of the United States, 1915–1940," doctoral dissertation, Southern Baptist Theological Seminary, 1949, 286.

[17] Louisville *Western Recorder*, July 26, 1928.

[18] El Paso *Times*, Oct. 20, 1928.

[19] In Florida, in 1928, 215 out of 365 meetings held under League auspices were conducted in churches; in Oklahoma, 200 out of 220; in Virginia, 224 out of 297; and, in Alabama, 80 out of 100. Eight out of thirteen state League superintendents in the South were clergymen. *The Anti-Saloon League Year Book, 1929*, ed. Ernest H. Cherrington (Westerville, Ohio, 1929), 87, 95, 135, 149, 181–82. On September 23, 1928, which it designated as Temperance Sunday, the League distributed anti-Smith pamphlets among approximately 30,000 Protestant congregations throughout the nation; sermons sup-

port: United States Senators Furnifold Simmons of North Carolina, and J. Thomas Heflin of Alabama, former United States Senator Robert L. Owen of Oklahoma, and former United States Representative William D. Upshaw of Georgia, for example. But these were exceptions. For, as the El Paso *Times* observed, "the leaders of the Democratic Party in the south are not bolting."[20] At the Asheville conference a reporter noted that, "save for Dr. Barton, and the Bishops of the Methodist Episcopal Church, South, being Bishop Cannon, Bishop H. M. Du Bose, Bishop Edwin D. Mouzon, and Dr. E. O. Watson, editor of the [Episcopalian] Southern Churchman . . . few of those present were recognized as outstanding leaders."[21] A contributor to the Memphis *Commercial Appeal* concluded that it was a contest "between preachers and politicians."[22] "Southern ministers seem to think they are divinely commissioned to defeat the Democratic Party," a Texan complained.[23]

It seems proper to identify the Southern Baptist and Methodist denominations as the moving force in the anti-Smith Democratic movement, through their leaders, convocations, agencies, and their press—and with enthusiastic rank-and-file clerical support. The authoritative Nashville *Christian Advocate* acknowledged that "our [Southern Methodist] Church has entered vigorously into the battle for prohibition," in league with the Southern Baptists.[24] Bishops Sam H. Hay,

---

porting Hoover's candidacy were part of the observance in many of these churches. The League later proclaimed October 28 Good Citizenship Sunday, when congregations were urged to emphasize the importance of voting. (New Orleans *Times-Picayune*, Sept. 23, Oct. 1, 1928.)

[20] El Paso *Times*, July 14, 1928.

[21] Asheville *Citizen*, July 18, 1928.

[22] Memphis *Commercial Appeal*, Nov. 4, 1928.

[23] El Paso *Times*, Sept. 12, 1928.

[24] Nashville *Christian Advocate*, Aug. 3, 1928. During the campaign, the Southern Methodist Board of Temperance and Social Service circulated "hundreds of thousands" of copies of a speech by Bishop Cannon entitled "Prohibition Repeal Unthinkable." (Watson, *Bishop Cannon's Own Story*, 442.) Senator Carter Glass bitterly criticized the secular press bureau of the

W. B. Beuchamp, and John M. Moore published assurances that "the entire Southern Methodist church will oppose Governor Smith."[25] The Arkansas *Baptist Advance* warned that any Baptist leader who dared endorse Smith "breaks ranks and declares himself out of harmony with the Arkansas Baptist Convention, the Southern Baptist Convention and the vast majority of Baptist pastors and other Baptist leaders. Not only that, but he also very seriously discounts his own standing as a Baptist."[26] The Reverend J. Frank Norris threatened to expose and disgrace "a small Baptist group pussyfooting and compromising on Al Smith."[27] Indeed the campaign was one of the few ventures of the decade to draw irascible fundamentalists such as Norris, William Bell Riley, Mordecai F. Hamm, John Roach Straton, and Billy Sunday into common cause with such southern denominational leaders as the Methodist bishops, and the presidents of Southern Methodist University, the Southern Baptist Theological Seminary, the Southwestern Baptist Theological Seminary, and Baylor University. Only a great crisis—or what was construed to be such —could have accomplished this.[28] "Ministers of all denominations fighting gloriously," Norris reported during a west Texas tour. His own speeches lasted "usually two hours, occasionally three," and "never ended without a religious appeal."[29] Bishop Cannon's biographer declares that ministers were on the platform "at virtually every anti-Smith meeting";[30] Can-

---

Methodist Episcopal Church, South, for distributing a press release accusing him and others of "betrayal of the prohibition cause for the sake of a purely partisan victory." (Memphis *Commercial Appeal*, Oct. 15, 1928.)

[25] El Paso *Times*, Oct. 2, 1928.

[26] Little Rock *Baptist Advance*, July 26, 1928.

[27] Fort Worth *Fundamentalist*, Sept. 28, 1928.

[28] A Georgia Baptist rejoiced that "ten of the twelve bishops of the Southern Methodist Church, ninety per cent of the Baptist ministers," and a "predominance of leadership in every Protestant denomination in the Southern states" were supporting Hoover. (Jackson *Baptist Record*, Aug. 16, 1928.)

[29] Fort Worth *Fundamentalist*, Sept. 28, Nov. 9, 1928.

[30] Virginius Dabney, *Dry Messiah: The Life of Bishop Cannon* (New York, 1949), 184.

non's personal role is stressed by Edmund A. Moore, who credits Hoover's showing in the South to him "more than anyone else."[31]

Although southern Democratic party leaders seldom defended Smith's views on prohibition, they otherwise praised his qualifications, and decried efforts to arouse religious prejudice against him. They also put to use an appeal which had been often tested in the past: equating disloyalty to the party with disloyalty to the South and its tradition of white supremacy. United States Senator Joseph Ransdell of Louisiana pleaded for white solidarity to avert "a return to the fraud and violence of Reconstruction days."[32] Governor Theodore G. Bilbo issued a special proclamation to the people of Mississippi charging that Hoover as Secretary of Commerce had assigned white girls "to work as secretaries and stenographers for negro bosses and forced them to use the same towels, soap, and rest rooms with negroes. . . ."[33] Bilbo also publicized a rumor, often retold, that Hoover once danced with Mary Booze, prominent Mississippi Negro Republican.[34] "I'd rather cut my arm off than to vote for a man who don't know the difference between a white man and a negro," exclaimed Tennessee Senator Kenneth D. McKellar.[35] The South would "never forget" those who forsook her "in her hour of need," a Texas editor served notice.[36] Even politicians of little acumen or experience well understood the force of such appeals.

But the preachers needed no instruction on handicaps and advantages, or in the art of public persuasion. This became evident when the Asheville conference took pains to dissociate itself from the Republican party, and portrayed itself as a defender of ancient ideals of the South and the Democratic

[31] Moore, *A Catholic Runs for President*, 169.
[32] New Orleans *Times-Picayune*, Oct. 28, 1928.
[33] *Ibid.*, Oct. 29, 1928.
[34] El Paso *Times*, Oct. 25, 1928.
[35] Memphis *Commercial Appeal*, Oct. 6, 1928.
[36] El Paso *Times*, Nov. 7, 1928.

party. "The one thing in this campaign I resent more than anything else," declared one Methodist preacher, "is the effort of those north of the Mason and Dixon line to make us take anything they serve."[37] Rank-and-file attachment to prohibition afforded the anti-Smith Democrats their greatest opportunity. For many voters it was enough to know that Smith was a "wet." Many campaigners dwelt on the extent of the candidate's personal addiction: "I am reliably informed," the editor of the South Carolina *Baptist Courier* reported, "that he drinks every day, and the number of his cocktails and highballs is variously estimated at from four to eight."[38]

It should be emphasized that only on the prohibition issue was there unanimity in the anti-Smith ranks, and that many churchmen campaigned exclusively on this—President Charles C. Selecman of Southern Methodist University, President E. Y. Mullins of the Southern Baptist Theological Seminary, and Bishop Horace M. Du Bose, for example.[39] Others inveighed also against Tammany Hall and Smith's urban, recent-immigrant background, but refrained from discussing his religious faith. Still others—including some prominent clerical leaders —publicly proclaimed that Smith's Catholicism disqualified him for the presidency. This latter point was sometimes argued on a comparatively high and dispassionate plane, and it would be unjust to stigmatize as bigots all who raised it.[40] But the corporate churches and their spokesmen cannot be absolved from complicity in the smear campaign often attributed to the Ku-Klux Klan fringe of Protestantism. Lacking coercive ecclesiastical powers, denominational leaders could only exhort; in

[37] *Ibid.*, Oct. 10, 1928. As Joe B. Frantz points out, "the problem . . . was to convince Southern voters that a bolt was not a bolt. The tack taken was that a true Democrat would vote against Smith. . . ." (Frantz, "A Historian Looks Back to '28.")

[38] Greenville, South Carolina, *Baptist Courier*, June 7, 1928.

[39] Shreveport *Journal*, Nov. 7, 1928; Memphis *Commercial Appeal*, Nov. 5, 1928; Nashville *Christian Advocate*, Aug. 3, 1928.

[40] For example, the Oklahoma *Baptist Messenger*, Aug. 28, 1928. On this point, see Miller, *American Protestantism and Social Issues*, 48–62.

their efforts to persuade, they resorted to common electioneering techniques—including sometimes a resort to religious and racial bigotry.

"Romist" and "Papist" were synonyms for "Roman Catholic" in the campaign, while Governor Smith's ceremonial kiss of a papal legate's ring, in 1927, became a gesture of temporal submission to the Pope.[41] "If Al Smith had been president at that time the performance would have taken place in the White House or the capitol, and the president of the United States would have knelt before the papal legate and kissed his ring as he sat on a throne under a canopy of stars and stripes mingled with the emblem of the pope's temporal power," a contributor to the Kentucky Baptist *Western Recorder* conjectured.[42] The South Carolina *Baptist Courier* published a warning—attributed to President Hayes's Secretary of the Navy, Richard W. Thompson—that "such a man, whether priest or layman, high or low, is necessarily inimical to the government and political institutions of the United States government; with him, his oath of allegiance is worth no more than the paper upon which it is written."[43] The Tennessee *Baptist and Reflector* feared that state secrets might "be divulged through the priest to whom Smith confesses, and, of course, they would then not stop short of the pope, who is king of the Catholic world." One contributor to this paper charged that Catholics "have murdered Baptists and Protestants by the thousands, if not by the millions," and that "three of our presidents have been assassinated, and it is understood that every one of them fell at the hands of Catholics. I have never heard a statement to the contrary."[44] In a speech at El Paso, the Reverend J. W. Hunt, president of Methodist-

---

[41] See James H. Smylie, "The Roman Catholic Church, the State, and Al Smith," *Church History*, XXIX (1960), 321–43.

[42] Louisville *Western Recorder*, Aug. 30, 1928.

[43] Greenville, South Carolina, *Baptist Courier*, Jan. 26, 1928.

[44] Quoted in Memphis *Commercial Appeal*, Sept. 30, 1928.

operated McMurry College, inveighed against having a "Catholic shrine in the White House," and warned that Smith was "listening to foreign influences." Before a Lubbock audience, President Hunt declared that the "chicken stealing, crapshooting, bootlegging negro crowd" supported Smith, whom he assailed as a "dirty, drunken, bum."[45]

Few journals exercised so little restraint as the Mississippi *Baptist Record*, weekly organ of the state convention. One article discussed a Catholic plot to " 'take charge of the politics of this country and thereby dominate the world' (This is a recent private declaration of a priest.)"[46] The *Record* told of an unidentified Jackson woman who had been obliged to vote for a candidate she opposed in a recent election "because her priest had told her to do it," and of a Vicksburg Negro Catholic's being directed by his priest to vote for Smith. "If the word of a Catholic priest can be believed," an editorial averred, "the negroes of Mississippi are being organized by the Catholic hierarchy to vote for Smith."[47] A contributor to the *Record* portrayed Smith as a scorner of Protestant virtue and motherhood: "Smith does not (as a good Catholic) believe in, nor does he recognize the laws of our country regarding the marriage relation. He, therefore, looks upon my mother and my wife and every other Protestant mother and wife as prostitutes and our children as bastards."[48] It is indicative that this slanderous appeal was also invoked by a leader of such standing as Bishop Cannon: "Is it intolerant or bigoted," Cannon asked, "to refuse to agree that Romanism has no [the?] right to pass judgment upon the validity of marriages performed by Protestant ministers or by the State, and thus brand as adul-

---

[45] El Paso *Times*, Oct. 26, 1928; Lubbock *Avalanche*, Nov. 1, 1928.
[46] B. H. Copass, "Al Smith and Company Throw Down the Gauntlet," in Jackson *Baptist Record*, Mar. 1, 1928.
[47] "The Question of Motives," *ibid.*, Aug. 23, 1928.
[48] G. C. Hodge, "Stewards of a Nation, or Why We Should Vote for Hoover," *ibid.*, Aug. 16, 1928.

terers those who have contracted marriages made without the sanction of Romanism, and as a consequence brands children of such marriages as bastards?"[49]

Thus was the crusade waged, a crusade which led to a sensational triumph. It was unusual for Hoover to carry Tennessee, Oklahoma, Kentucky, West Virginia, and Maryland. But his victories in Texas, Virginia, North Carolina, and Florida were more surprising since the latter belonged to a ten-state "solid South" bloc which had voted Democratic in every previous national election since Reconstruction.[50] Among the more tumultuous victory celebrations was one at the Fort Worth First Baptist Church. During the rally the state anti-Smith Democratic campaign manager presented an engraved watch to the Reverend J. Frank Norris, whom he cited for doing "more than any other man in Texas to carry the state for Hoover."[51] A more sedate convocation at the Dallas University Club feted Protestant clergymen collectively. James H. (Cyclone) Davis recited limericks ridiculing "Smith, Raskob, rum, Tammany, the Pope and the alien"; S.M.U. President Selecman assured the five hundred banqueters that "preachers will always enter politics to fight liquor."[52]

---

[49] Dabney, *Dry Messiah*, 186. Edmund A. Moore cautions that "in discussing bigotry, it is all too easy to suppose that what happened in the South was unique to that section. Actually much of what happened in the South was typical of what occurred elsewhere." (Moore, *A Catholic Runs for President*, 172.) It does appear, however, that such appeals were used with more effect in the South and border area than in other areas.

[50] See Key, *Southern Politics in State and Nation:* "Minute examination of the relation between the distribution of the Al Smith vote and the Negro population amply sustains the major thesis: that the diehard Democratic strength in 1928 centered in counties with high proportions of Negroes" (p. 328). On the other hand, "counties with large urban centers tended generally to be more Republican than were rural counties with comparable proportions of Negro population" (p. 328). "Thus, not only high Negro population ratios were associated with Democratic steadfastness. A complex of factors —ruralism, cotton growing, plantation organization, intense Reconstruction memories—as well as anxieties about the racial equilibrium characterized the Democratic areas" (p. 329).

[51] Fort Worth *Fundamentalist*, Nov. 9, 1928.

[52] Dallas *Morning News*, Nov. 10, 11, 1928.

Yet the victory was not without cost and sacrifice. For, as the campaign progressed, the anticlerical reaction rose to proportions almost surely without precedent in the South. A Georgia Baptist protested that the "pledging [by the Southern Baptist Convention] of the votes of 3,700,000 members of the convention is without any foundation . . . in the laws of the association, and merits the condemnation of all right thinking Baptists of the South";[53] the Birmingham *News* assailed the convention's anti-Smith "covenant" as "among the boldest efforts known, since the constitution was adopted, to impose the will of theologians upon their co-religionists in purely civil affairs."[54] A group of eighty-three prominent Southern Methodist laymen decried "the dragging of our beloved church into politics," and complained that "some of our church papers have become political periodicals more bitter and intolerant than many secular papers."[55] Senator Carter Glass belittled those "who would change my church to the Methodist Republican Church, South."[56] A typical critic complained to the Memphis *Commercial Appeal* that southern clergymen had "quit preaching religion and gone to preaching politics," and had thus "cheapened their calling and profession . . . and they have even cheapened themselves." He urged adjustments in salaries to comport with talent and performance.[57]

All in all, the reaction was one which disparaged the clerical office as well as clergymen themselves, one which implied a general status deterioration in the ministry. And other evi-

[53] El Paso *Times*, June 8, 1928.
[54] Quoted in Birmingham *Alabama Baptist*, June 7, 1928.
[55] New Orleans *Times-Picayune*, Oct. 6, 1928. Two Southern Methodist bishops—Collins Denny and Warren A. Candler—vehemently protested the involvement of the church in the campaign. Candler condemned as "a fatal blunder" the "intrusion of any Church, whether Protestant or Romish, into the arena of party politics." (New York *Times*, July 17, 1928; Alfred M. Pierce, *Giant Against the Sky: The Life of Bishop Warren Akin Candler* [Nashville, 1948], 220.)
[56] New York *Times*, Nov. 2, 1928.
[57] Memphis *Commercial Appeal*, Nov. 4, 1928.

dences in the period tended to support this implication. Thus, in 1927, the Southern Methodist College of Bishops recalled that "in times past our preachers were leaders of the people." The bishops warned that the education of the clergy had "not kept pace with the education of the people at large," that 32 per cent of the Southern Methodist clergy had not advanced in formal schooling beyond the elementary level.[58] The preparation of Baptist preachers was probably even less; enrollment in the three Southern Baptist theological seminaries declined from 1,496 in 1920–21 to 977 in 1929–30.[59] The strength of the antievolution movement in the South seemed as much attributable to the intellectual backwardness of the clergy as to any other factor. During the 1928 campaign, when John Jacob Raskob urged steps by Protestant laymen to curtail clerical anti-Smith activity, a Florida minister grumbled that "fifty years ago no Raskob nor any other Kob, would have dared to even think he could shut the preachers' mouths by threatening them with boycott of salary." The Floridian complained that clergymen were widely regarded as "hirelings" and "cowardlings."[60] The evidence suggests that the campaign of 1928 served both to degrade the southern clergy and to render explicit a decline already under way. The Chattanooga *Times* editorialized that "the effect on the political complexion of the South is not so serious as will be the loss of confidence, inevitably resulting, in the spiritual integrity of a large section of the Protestant ministry."[61]

[58] "An Episcopal Address: A Better Prepared Ministry," in Nashville *Christian Advocate*, June 24, 1927.

[59] Southern Baptist Sunday School Board, *Southern Baptist Handbook, 1921* (Nashville, 1921), 195, 231, 233; *Southern Baptist Handbook, 1930* (Nashville, 1930), 215.

[60] The Reverend E. L. Wessen, of Dade City, Florida. Jackson *Baptist Record*, Sept. 6, 1928. In their study of *Middletown*, in 1925, the Lynds noted an attitude of condescension toward the clergy, and that ministers were excluded from the Rotary Club, "which boasts that it includes all the leaders of the community. . . ." (Robert S. and Helen M. Lynd, *Middletown: A Study in Contemporary American Culture*, 350, 406.)

[61] Chattanooga *Times*, Nov. 7, 1928.

Nor did events after Hoover's inauguration seem much to vindicate the crusade. The Great Depression was not a promised fruit of the nonalcoholic millennium or a fitting reward for a people who had forsaken political precedent to uphold a great moral principle. Moreover, it became increasingly clear that national prohibition was not, after all, firmly established. "The spirit of the evangelical bodies in the South is being broken by economic depression, hostile propaganda and clumsy leadership," wrote a contributor to the *Alabama Baptist,* in the midst of the depression. "The growing disrespect shown all evangelical leaders, as they strive to lead, is one of the most disturbing aspects of the situation." A Presbyterian journal lamented that the Church, "considered as an organization —a machine which exists for the purpose of bringing in the kingdom of God—has not been functioning smoothly," that it was not "as forceful or authoritative as once in social, economic and political movements, or even in education, where it once led the way."[62]

Twice within the decade previous to 1928—in mobilizing public opinion during World War I, and in the antievolution crusade—southern clergymen assumed effective leadership in mass quasi-secular, quasi-religious movements. But the history of the South since 1928 affords no parallel—not during the crisis of the Great Depression, not during World War II or the Korean War, not in the current segregation crisis. On the eve of the 1960 campaign, the Southern Baptist Convention openly questioned the qualification of any Catholic for high public office, a viewpoint it had not officially acknowledged in 1928. Southern churchmen, principally Baptist and Church of Christ, proclaimed against Kennedy much as their predecessors proclaimed against Smith. Yet the similarities between 1960 and 1928 are more apparent than real. The Methodist hierarchy in the South remained relatively passive during the

[62] Rufus W. Weaver, "Our Evangelical Crisis," in Birmingham *Alabama Baptist,* Sept. 21, 1933; Nashville *Presbyterian Advance,* May 25, 1933.

1960 debate; the management of Nixon's southern campaign was in secular hands, and clerical endorsements were received more with apology than with elation; ministers rarely ventured from their pulpits to campaign in the manner of 1928. Notwithstanding the new respectability of the Republican party in the South, and the strong civil rights platform of the Democratic party, Kennedy attracted more southern electoral votes than Smith, or than Stevenson in either 1952 or 1956. In previous decades, a decline in church influence seemed evident in the movement away from prohibition. Heated clerical injunctions failed to forestall ratification of the Twenty-first Amendment in a majority of the southern states—or the subsequent abandonment of state-wide prohibition except in Mississippi. In 1963 a Danville, Virginia, newspaper scolded the churches in that city for their involvement in the racial crisis. As in many other localities, clergymen were advised that racial integration was a "secular problem."[63]

[63] Danville *Bee*, Sept. 14, 1963.

6

THE IMPACT OF THE DEPRESSION

The Great Depression unsettled the southern churches much as it unsettled secular institutions. Declining contributions forced retrenchments in budgets. Pledges went unmet, debts went unpaid. A general despondency stifled initiative. With national attention now fixed on survival, moreover, the concern of many churchmen seemed curiously misdirected. "How often," one historian marvels, "did the reader of the church press in the depression start an editorial or article entitled 'The Need of the Hour,' 'A Time of Crisis,' 'The President Must Lead,' 'Moral Issues in the Election,' 'The Stakes in the Election,' 'It is Time for the President to Act,' only to discover that, far from dealing with the economic crisis, it was concerned with prohibition!"[1] Yet, as Hoover's popularity waned, clergymen spoke less of their accomplishments in 1928.

[1] Miller, *American Protestantism and Social Issues*, 120.

Though the depression was not attributed to the liquor traffic as many past adversities had been, some fundamentalists interpreted it as an apocalyptic visitation brought on by worldliness. When asked for his views on the causes of the depression, one conservative Baptist tersely replied in one word: "Sin." Another Baptist opined that "the best thing men can do is to spread the Bible and to get it read and obeyed. This would be the end of hard times, of poverty, of unemployment, of injustice, or wrong, or war." "If all of us will fix our faith in God, strive to walk in His ways, keep His Commandments, and seek to help others and to avoid excessive extravagance and waste," exhorted a Southern Presbyterian journal, "we will before long find ourselves on the highway to peace and prosperity." The Reverend William Bell Riley woefully portrayed the depression as but a fulfillment of prophecy, an inexorable prelude to an "explosion that will leave the world filled with the fragments of human minds and bodies."[2]

Occasionally religious leaders grappled with critical economic needs in their communities. Few religious congregations found that they could "do much" about unemployment, however, even though the Richmond *Presbyterian of the South* thought that they could.[3] Some did organize substantial relief programs. The Lubbock First Baptist Church designated a "benevolence room" where food and clothing were received and disbursed, and a nondenominational Sunday school in Lubbock purchased food in wholesale lots for its needy members.[4] Far more ambitious was a program carried out in Fort Worth under the direction of J. Frank Norris. To a man of Norris' capacities, the hopelessness of the situation was only a challenge. By radio and telephone, through the press, and

[2] Lexington, Kentucky, *American Baptist*, Dec. 9, 23, 1931; Louisville *Christian Observer*, Apr. 20, 1932; Louisville *Western Recorder*, June 15, 1933.
[3] Richmond *Presbyterian of the South*, Jan. 20, 1932.
[4] Merton L. Dillon, "Religion in Lubbock," *Museum Journal* (Lubbock, Texas), V (1961), 483.

in face-to-face solicitations, he begged and cajoled donations. Cots and shower baths were installed in his church building and made available to the destitute. "Big stoves are kept red hot day and night for the great army of homeless," he announced during the bleak winter of 1932–33. His congregation also prepared and served food; by April 1933 they had distributed 47,737 free meals, 33,390 gallons of milk, and 5,327 items of clothing. Norris promised that "any case of real sickness" brought to his attention would receive competent medical treatment and that medication would be provided upon a doctor's prescription. Rejoicing for once at the "overwhelmingly gratifying" response of his community, he praised "Jews, Gentiles, Catholics, Protestants, saints and sinners" alike for their generosity.[5] It was a strange role into which Norris was cast, but the times were as unusual as the role.

Only infrequently did clergymen relate local needs to national policy before the advent of the New Deal. In 1932, as in 1928, the Southern Baptist Convention resolved to support for the presidency and lesser offices "only such candidates and nominees as believe in and support prohibition" and to oppose all others.[6] But the convention's action this time achieved few results. Republicans refused to espouse the Eighteenth Amendment forthrightly; the Democratic Convention unequivocably demanded that national prohibition be ended. "The position taken by both candidates of the major political parties [on prohibition] is disappointing," the Oklahoma *Baptist Messenger* grumbled. Like almost all southern religious papers in 1932, the *Alabama Baptist* did not "pretend to advise any one how to vote"; it acknowledged "many other considerations in the present presidential campaign besides the wet and dry issue," and conceded after the election that the *zeitgeist* was "in full swing against prohibition." "Perhaps

---

[5] Fort Worth *Fundamentalist*, Dec. 23, 1932, Jan. 6, Mar. 31, 1933.
[6] Southern Baptist Convention, *Annual, 1932* (Nashville, 1932), 98.

no thoughtful man agrees with *all* in the platform he supports," the South Carolina *Baptist Courier* concluded.[7]

Though the Eighteenth Amendment was clearly a hopeless cause, and though there was little to suggest that it elevated morality, few southern churchmen acknowledged its failure. And few forgave President Roosevelt for advocating repeal. Nevertheless, the interest of church councils veered toward other reforms as the New Deal got under way. "We may not march in the Wet Parade with our courageous President or agree with him in his big Army and Navy program," a committee of the Alabama State Baptist Convention declared in December 1933. "But we can keep step with him in his efforts to maintain World Peace and achieve disarmament; to spread wealth; secure higher wages and shorter hours for labor; abolish child labor; to promote a planned industry to prevent unemployment; insurance and old age security; and other measures of social justice."[8] The 1933 Southern Baptist Convention pledged the new President "the support of our Baptist people in his earnest efforts to relieve the distress of millions of men now without employment"; delegates shunted aside a committee's expression of "great concern upon the unusual and extraordinary grants of power to the President by Congress." The convention the following year lauded Roosevelt for "splendid leadership to economic and industrial recovery, and more particularly for the many ways you are bringing Christian ideals to bear upon our national and world problems."[9] At their quadrennial General Conference in 1934 Southern Methodists incorporated into the church *Discipline* the new Social Creed of the Federal Council of Churches. In so doing they espoused many New Deal objectives—"social

[7] Oklahoma City *Baptist Messenger*, Aug. 25, 1932; Birmingham *Alabama Baptist*, Sept. 1, 1932, July 20, 1933; Greenville, South Carolina, *Baptist Courier*, July 14, 1932.

[8] Birmingham *Alabama Baptist*, Dec. 7, 1933.

[9] Southern Baptist Convention, *Annual, 1933* (Nashville, 1933), 23, 104; Louisville *Western Recorder*, June 14, 1934.

planning and control in the economic process," "the right of employees and employers alike to organize for collective bargaining and social action," and "social insurance against sickness, accident, want in old age, and unemployment." "Conservatism and individualism have been more or less pushed aside by a large degree of liberalism and a pronounced form of socialism," the Methodist bishops observed.[10]

Southern Protestants joined others in criticizing *laissez-faire* capitalism as it functioned before the depression. Before the election of 1932 a Presbyterian perceived that "business leaders have been neither so wise nor so disinterested in interpreting economic laws as the astronomers have been in reading the laws of the stars."[11] As Roosevelt prepared to take office, the Nashville *Christian Advocate* proclaimed that old economic axioms were "utterly invalidated" and "could never be restored."[12] "The old capitalistic system failed," declared the *Alabama Baptist*, in August 1933; "the whole banking system failed; the government itself fairly tottered, and there is no where else to go except with the President. . . ."[13] Renouncing all systems based on competition and profit, a conference of five hundred young Methodists, meeting at Lynchburg, Virginia, in 1937, hoped for "the ultimate establishment of a world economic and social order in which service shall be the motive, co-operation the means, and universal equality and plenty the end of all production."[14] Stirred by the Nye Committee's sensational investigations, in 1934, the Southern Methodist Temperance and Social Service Committee flayed "those selfish business interests and corporations which endeavor to stir up strife among races and hatred among

[10] Methodist Episcopal Church, South, General Conference, *Journal, 1934* (Nashville, 1934), 50–51, 368.
[11] Henry Wade Du Bose, "The Present Crisis and the Cause of Christ," in Louisville *Christian Observer*, Oct. 26, 1932.
[12] Nashville *Christian Advocate*, Jan. 6, 1933.
[13] Birmingham *Alabama Baptist*, Aug. 17, 1933.
[14] Nashville *Christian Advocate*, Aug. 13, 1937.

nations that they may profit by the sale of arms and munitions
. . . and exploit the common people by doubling, and in
many instances quadrupling, the price of the actual necessities
of life in the form of food and clothing." The committee
demanded that material wealth "be 'conscripted' along with
man-power" in any future war.[15]

Fundamentalism was now often derided as a mainstay of
economic reaction. "Whenever there has been an earnest
effort to interpret and apply the teachings of Jesus to the
solution of economic problems," a Southern Presbyterian
mused, ". . . one hears voices . . . asking 'why aren't
preachers satisfied to preach the "Gospel," and let other
people alone?' "[16] "The captains of finance wanted a simple
gospel," recalled the *Alabama Baptist*; "the preacher was to
save souls, comfort the sorrowing, bury the dead. But the
minute he thrust his gospel rapier into crooked finance, into
government graft, into individual greed and avarice he was to
be dislodged from the sacred stand."[17] The Nashville *Christian Advocate* scorned the "corporation manager who is very
zealous for the simple gospel. The preacher is to keep his eye
on heaven, while the corporation is to keep its eye on the main
chance in this mundane sphere." This Methodist journal identified those desiring "false profits in business" as the chief foes
of the social gospel. It goaded churches to manifest a social
concern beyond "safe and self-righteous" condemnations of
smoking and drinking; it inquired whether any church "has
expressed itself against a condition in which a million and
more tenant families in the cotton belt eke out a wretched
existence in poverty and illiteracy?"[18] A Kentucky Baptist
found that social evils flourished most in areas where ortho-

[15] Methodist Episcopal Church, South, General Conference, *Journal*, 1934, 151.
[16] Richmond *Presbyterian of the South*, Feb. 13, 1934.
[17] Birmingham *Alabama Baptist*, Nov. 9, 1933.
[18] Nashville *Christian Advocate*, Sept. 1, 22, 1933, July 16, 1937.

doxy and evangelism were most stressed. In the manner that his co-religionists attributed "superstition, ignorance and low moral ideals in Latin America to Roman Catholicism," he placed major blame on his denominaton for the "far from Christian" social attitudes which prevailed in the South.[19]

Revisions in worship hymnals reflected the changing times. One student found trends in Methodist hymnology away "from appeals to 'other-worldliness' and 'prospects of heaven' to the ideal of eternal life as self-forgetfulness in the service of God," "from an extreme individualistic interest in religion to that of a more collective and social interest."[20] His analysis came after a 1935 revision of the official hymn book used in both the Southern and Northern Methodist Churches. A major purpose of the revision was to give new emphasis to the social gospel; one member of the editing committee lamented that "some wonderful features of this gospel cannot well be put to verse—as, for instance, the eighteen hour day and the second-hand clothing shop and store."[21] Calls to action took precedence over chantings on death and perdition. One new selection pledged to "bring in the day of brotherhood and end the night of wrong"; another begged Providence to "save us from weak resignation to the evils we deplore."[22] Some Methodists must have felt such misgivings as were voiced by a Southern Presbyterian after a similar revision of his church hymnal in 1928. "My first feeling was that the committee had deleted the great hymns portraying the awfulness and majesty of God, and the horrors of the Cross!" he exclaimed. And he had not been "reassured by fuller examination."[23] "Many of

[19] Louisville *Western Recorder*, Aug. 10, 1933.

[20] Benjamin Franklin Crawford, *Changing Conceptions of Religion, as Revealed in One Hundred Years of Methodist Hymnology, 1836–1935* (Carnegie, Pa., 1939), 158, 163.

[21] Edwin Holt Hughes, "The Hymnal Revisers at Work," in Nashville *Christian Advocate*, Oct. 6, 1933.

[22] *The Methodist Hymnal* (Nashville, 1935), Hymn Nos. 267, 279.

[23] Charlotte *Presbyterian Standard*, Apr. 18, 1928.

ie modern hymn books seem to give preference to hymns by Unitarians," another southerner complained.[24]

In few denominations was the quickening of reform interest so evident as in the Southern Presbyterian Church. More theologically oriented than Methodists or Baptists, Presbyterians had shown little previous concern for social causes. The General Assembly had affiliated with the Federal Council of Churches before World War I. But the assembly refrained from adopting or endorsing the council's controversial Social Creed. Even so, the affiliation with the Federal Council was never popular among rank-and-file communicants. Finally, after much debate, the 1931 assembly voted to withdraw.[25] The General Assembly had promulgated a mildly phrased "United Declaration on Christian Faith and Social Service" in 1914, and on other occasions had explicitly condemned Sabbath desecration, lynching, drinking, war, and many less obvious evils.[26] Unlike the Southern Baptists and Methodists, however, the Presbyterians had established no social service commission to direct agitation on such matters. For this as well as more fundamental reasons of principle, they avoided official involvement in the campaign of 1928.

It was thus a marked departure when many Presbyterian leaders emerged as champions of the New Deal. Not atypical was an Alabama clergyman who rejoiced that "the unrestrained capitalistic order seems to have passed from the American scene by common consent, and it has not been given even a low class funeral."[27] "If you will compare some of the underlying principles of the New Deal with some of the principles of the Old Book," President Walter L. Lingle of Davidson College reasoned, "you will find that they are very

[24] Louisville *Christian Observer*, Aug. 8, 1928.
[25] Presbyterian Church in the United States, General Assembly, *Minutes, 1931* (Richmond, Va., 1931), 47. The General Assembly of 1941 voted to reaffiliate with the Federal Council of Churches. (Presbyterian Church in the United States, General Assembly, *Minutes, 1941* [Richmond, 1941], 63.)
[26] See Chap. 2.
[27] Richmond *Presbyterian of the South*, July 11, 1934.

similar."[28] Another Presbyterian complained that the pre-depression economic order had neglected "the obligation of the Christian to the community."[29] Church convocations assembled to ponder social conditions. One such conference of two hundred Presbyterian clergymen met at Montreat, North Carolina, in the autumn of 1933, and for a week deliberated such topics as "The Practical Applications of the Teachings of Jesus to the Problems of Today," "Christianity and the Depression," and "Christianity and the Race Problem." Before adjourning, the conferees affirmed that Christian principles would "transform our economic order by placing the motive of service above that of self-seeking, by substituting the method of co-operation for that of ruthless competition. . . ."[30]

Similar statements were officially promulgated by presbyteries and synods. The Alabama Synod of 1933 resolved that "much of the suffering of our time is traceable to an inadequate understanding of the teachings of Christ regarding human relationships, and to a pagan conception of property";[31] the Virginia Synod stressed "the obligation of the Church to take cognizance of existing moral and social problems, [and] to study and endeavor to understand their causes, effect, and cure . . .";[32] the Georgia Synod ridiculed "that attitude as expressed by Froude when he said that the spokesmen of religion should 'leave the present world to the men of business and the devil.' "[33] Virginia Presbyterians led the way in 1932 in setting up a special synodical committee on social and moral welfare.[34] Similar committees were established by the Georgia, Alabama, and Louisiana Synods in 1933, the Oklahoma Synod in 1934, and the Tennessee Synod in

[28] Louisville *Christian Observer*, Jan. 24, 1934.
[29] Richmond *Presbyterian of the South*, Jan. 3, 1934.
[30] Louisville *Christian Observer*, Sept. 13, Oct. 4, 1933.
[31] *Ibid.*, Nov. 1, 1933.
[32] *Ibid.*, Oct. 4, 1933.
[33] Richmond *Presbyterian of the South*, Nov. 27, 1935.
[34] Louisville *Christian Observer*, Oct. 4, 1933.

1935.[35] Meanwhile, the General Assembly debated whether to sponsor such a group. Assembly delegates voted to do so in 1933, but then rescinded their action and even expunged it from the record.[36] But the assembly the next year acted again and this time held its ground. The new Permanent Committee on Social and Moral Welfare was instructed to report annually, although its findings would become denominational pronouncements only as proclaimed by the assembly.[37] Persistent complaints about the welfare committee were of little avail. "Why should we leave our divinely given task to become embroiled like many of our sister churches in the bitter controversies now raging in the economic, political and social realms . . .?" asked twenty-three delegates to the General Assembly of 1937. Their protest was curtly rejected "since as a whole it is simply a blanket contradiction of the conclusion of the General Assembly on this question."[38]

Early in the decade the Concord Presbytery begged the General Assembly to "reaffirm the historic testimony of our Church as to the moral danger of card playing and dancing and theatre-going, or failing that . . . rescind former actions advising against these forms of indulgence." For many years the assembly refused to comply. Acknowledging "the subtle temptations presented through the appeals of present-day recreational and social life," it prescribed only "a careful searching of heart and training tastes, under the sought guidance of the Holy Spirit in these matters"; communicants were vaguely exhorted to "face squarely the issues presented" and to "arrive at character-making decisions." Not until 1945 was a forthright clarification handed down. In that year the assembly finally affirmed that "amusements usually listed as worldly—dancing, theatre-going, and card playing—are not inherently

[35] *Ibid.*, Oct. 25, Nov. 1, Dec. 6, 1933, Oct. 9, 23, 1935.
[36] *Ibid.*, May 31, June 7, 1933.
[37] *Ibid.*, June 6, 1934.
[38] Presbyterian Church in the United States, General Assembly, *Minutes, 1937* (Richmond, Va., 1937), 60, 75.

evil, nor do they always lead to evil." "Instead of condemning amusements which may be innocent," declared this highest church tribunal, "we should rather condemn the evil motives which sometimes pervert them. The 'principles and practices that mar Christian character and influence' have their roots in the heart and may be, and often are, manifested as dangerously in business, politics, race relations, and in national selfishness and isolationism, as in amusements."[39] The changed code of conduct could hardly have been expressed more explicitly.

Thus moved the tide in one of the more conservative southern bodies. With some reason, the Southern Presbyterian *Christian Observer* cautioned in 1935 that churches were "on the way to making this [social reform] the principal objective of their effort."[40] But few if any Presbyterian clergymen intruded so boldly into secular spheres as the renowned pastor of the Fort Worth First Baptist Church. "Why somebody cries 'socialism,' 'socialism!'" sneered J. Frank Norris during a Sunday sermon in which he defended the New Deal. "To hell with your socialism or what ever you want to call it! People are starving!" (His congregation applauded.)[41]

Of all major groups, however, the Methodists clamored most persistently for reform. The southern church allocated substantial sums to the work of its militant-minded Temperance and Social Service Board. Although this agency's first concern was prohibition, it now gave consistent attention to race relations, conditions of labor, and other social ills. Its liberal views were mirrored in church pronouncements, in Sunday school literature, in the denominational press, and in the programs of ever-more-frequent retreats and study conferences. When the Temperance and Social Service Board was discon-

[39] Presbyterian Church in the United States, General Assembly, *Minutes, 1930,* 36, 83; *Minutes, 1945* (Richmond, Va., 1945), 143.
[40] Louisville *Christian Observer*, May 22, 1935.
[41] Fort Worth *Fundamentalist*, Mar. 23, 1934. Norris soon turned bitterly against Roosevelt and the New Deal.

tinued in 1934, its functions were enlarged and assigned to other bureaus; for example, the General Board of Lay Activities was directed to emphasize "the gospel of Christ, as it affects industrial, racial, and international relations." "The Church has a responsibility in world reconstruction which it cannot and must not vacate," the bishops reiterated in 1934. The last regular Southern Methodist General Conference, in 1938, made clear that the church must always "pass judgment on social institutions as well as individuals."[42] Nor did unification with Northern Methodism moderate the trend. "What may we reasonably believe to be God's design in raising up the Methodist preachers?" asked the bishops of the newly united church, in 1939. "To reform the continent and spread scriptural holiness over these lands," was their rhetorical rejoinder.[43] This historic query and response was first given at the founding conference of American Methodism, at Baltimore, late in the eighteenth century. The charge remained the same. But the times and the meaning were vastly different.

Of course reform did not enlist the sympathy of all believers in the Methodist or any other denomination; the utterances of bishops, editors, and church convocations were not utterances of Protestantism at large. Nor were most such pronouncements proclaimed as dogma. The usual nondogmatic statements and resolutions served an educational purpose to the extent that they were expounded in the religious press, in Sunday school literature, and from pulpits; presumably they reflected broad trends and tolerance ranges in opinion. But they did not *per se* speak the concern of a majority. It seems certain that preachers spoke less of reform than seminary professors and denominational bureaucrats. On into the 1960's depravity and grace remained popular pulpit themes, especially among the Baptists.

[42] Methodist Episcopal Church, South, General Conference, *Journal, 1934,* 216, 360; *Journal, 1938* (Nashville, 1938), 230.
[43] The Methodist Church, Uniting Conference of 1939, *Journal* (Nashville, 1939), 158.

Nor did religious reformers escape embarrassing rebuffs as enthusiasm for the New Deal waned. In 1935 the Presbyterian Synod of Alabama refused to approve a statement "so far reaching and of such serious import" as that drafted by its Social Relations Committee.[44] The Georgia Synod reacted similarly to a report of its equivalent committee the following year.[45] The 1937 Southern Presbyterian General Assembly approved certain recommendations of its Permanent Committee on Social and Moral Welfare, but accepted other parts of the group's report only "as information"; this was a procedure followed in subsequent years.[46] Presbyterian social welfare committees minimized economic reform and race relations as the decade wore on. In 1935, for example, the Louisiana committee centered its wrath on the "low ethical standards revealed by many who hold public office and the lax attitude toward honest elections";[47] in 1936 the Virginia committee stressed the problems of crime, liquor, and war.[48] Yet the Southern Presbyterian Church did not repudiate its broad commitment to social amelioration as some members hoped it would. One disgruntled presbytery begged the General Assembly of 1947 to clarify that "the Presbyterian Church in the United States has not taken any action approving miscegenation, the removal of restrictions on housing segregation, the activities of the Fair Employment Practices Commission, the closed shop, or the abrogation of the American system of free enterprise."[49] The overture went unanswered.

Religious reformers probably experienced their greatest defeats in the Southern Baptist Convention. Indeed, at the close of the decade the convention seemed only slightly more

[44] Louisville *Christian Observer*, Nov. 6, 1935.

[45] *Ibid.*, Nov. 4, 1936.

[46] Presbyterian Church in the United States, General Assembly, *Minutes,* 1937, 37.

[47] Louisville *Christian Observer*, Dec. 11, 1935.

[48] *Ibid.*, Nov. 11, 1936.

[49] Presbyterian Church in the United States, General Assembly, *Minutes,* 1947 (Richmond, Va., 1947), 38.

conscious of social needs than before the advent of the New Deal. For several years a debate raged over a proposal to establish a denominational social research bureau. As envisioned, the agency would define major social problems, compile data, and suggest remedies (e.g., on the "social, educational, and religious problems of the Negro"); it would function independently of the conservative social service commission, and would not be tied to "any existing agency of the Convention to such an extent *that the most objective sort of studies might be interfered with.*" Denominational publications would be encouraged to use the bureau's findings in a vast program of social education. "With our great numbers, and the way in which Southern Baptist interests ramify into every aspect of the life of the South," a sponsoring group declared, "we as a people should take the leadership in a program of reconstruction that would inspire the whole of Christendom to seek to apply the gospel of Christ to all our social problems."[50] It was a project of grand scope.

The 1933 Southern Baptist Convention appointed a committee of five, headed by Edwin McNeill Poteat, Jr., of Wake Forest College, to prepare specific recommendations. When the group submitted a report favorable to such a program, however, final action was deferred.[51] A Texan ridiculed the bureau as a "smelling committee that would go around meddling with everybody and everybody's business" and which would duplicate efforts by the federal government to succor "mendicants and dead-beats." He taunted Poteat "to peddle your socialistic wares in the North, where there seems to be a more hospitable atmosphere for heresies, religious, social, and political."[52] From almost the beginning it was apparent that Poteat's supporters were in a minority. When the 1936 convention tabled the report, it in effect rejected the bureau.[53]

[50] Southern Baptist Convention, *Annual, 1935* (Nashville, n.d.), 57–58.
[51] Southern Baptist Convention, *Annual, 1933,* 188; *Annual, 1935,* 57.
[52] Louisville *Western Recorder,* June 27, July 4, 1935.
[53] Southern Baptist Convention, *Annual, 1936* (Nashville, n.d.), 38.

If conservative ascendancy in the convention required further demonstration, this came in 1937. That year the Reverend Charles R. Bell, Jr., of Anniston, Alabama, importuned the convention to endorse a series of statements on social questions beyond the innocuous ones submitted by the social service commission. After "peppery debate," the convention voted down Bell's resolutions calling for the regulation of child labor in mines and industry, upholding the right of labor to bargain collectively, and affirming that "human personality should take precedence over profits." On the other hand, it adopted "by vigorous vote" another clergyman's resolution deploring the use of tobacco. The convention also decried communistic encroachments in the United States and exhorted law enforcement officers to tolerate "no 'Red Flag' parade anywhere beneath the American flag."[54] A Baptist scholar concludes that editors of Baptist journals in the Southeast during this period were content "to celebrate the moral victories of former generations," that they "were not usually the inaugurators of, nor the leaders in, social reform," and that they "tended, in general, to reflect the views of the average layman on ethical issues."[55]

Yet the total impact of the depression on the churches was not registered in social pronouncements, in budgetary adjustments, or in local relief efforts. For the economic crisis and the recovery program cut across bounds of region and locality and combined with other forces to weaken sectionalism. The trend was manifest in many ways. Jim Crow color barriers wavered slightly in some southern communities; with the abolition of the two-thirds rule in the national Democratic Convention, in 1936, southerners relinquished their veto power over party nominations; the Tennessee Valley Authority,

[54] Southern Baptist Convention, *Annual, 1937* (Nashville, n.d.), 78; Shreveport *Baptist Message*, May 20, 1937; Oklahoma City *Baptist Messenger*, May 20, 1937; Macon, Georgia, *Christian Index*, May 27, 1937.
[55] Hill, "Ethical Emphases of the Baptist Editors in the Southeastern Region of the United States, 1915–1940," 290, 295.

mechanization, liberal farm credit, and efficient management lessened many eccentricities of southern agriculture. And, in Protestantism, the decade was an historic one of reconciliation. A new rapport developed between the Southern Baptist Convention and its northern counterpart; Presbyterians moved toward a national merger; northern and southern Methodists ended their century-old schism.

The Southern and Northern Baptist Conventions broke precedent in 1933, at Washington, D. C., when they assembled consecutively in the same city. Northern delegates attended sessions of the southern group; southerners participated in meetings of the northern body. At an informal joint session, the presidents of the two conventions dramatically clasped hands in a gesture of unity. The Oklahoma *Baptist Messenger* acclaimed this a "high day in American Baptist history" and rejoiced that there were "multitudes of Baptists in the Northern Convention who are as strict Baptists as their brethren in the South."[56] Once more at St. Louis, in 1936, the conventions met consecutively with similar displays of amity.[57] Not until 1964 would the two bodies convene in such manner again.

Of greater portent were the merger negotiations which commenced between Southern and Northern Presbyterians in 1937. Although these were not the first such consultations, they were more promising than any previously undertaken. Hopes for unification remained bright through the 1940's. When a specific proposal was finally submitted in 1954, however, it was defeated in the southern church. What might have been achieved in the 1930's could not be accomplished amidst sharpening racial frictions two decades later.[58]

[56] Oklahoma City *Baptist Messenger,* June 1, 1933.

[57] The Reverend A. J. Barton discussed the two joint meetings in the report which he submitted as chairman of the temperance and social service commission in 1941. (Southern Baptist Convention, *Annual, 1941* [Nashville, n.d.], 123–36.)

[58] Louisville *Christian Observer,* May 4, 1955; Nashville *Christian Advocate,* Feb. 10, 1955. This was the first time such a merger plan had actually been

A parallel effort in Methodism led rapidly to a merger in 1939. Opponents of union resisted the move as vigorously as they had a decade before. Bishop Warren A. Candler feared that a united church might "insist that our educational institutions admit equally both white and colored students";[59] another sectionalist served notice that "not every Southern delegate will consent to sit . . . with colored delegates" and that the "feelings of Southerners are sure to be hurt by insults from Northerners"; another alleged that "the Northern church membership is probably today composed of a larger percentage of foreign-born, children of foreign-born parents, Negroes and aliens, than any large Protestant denomination in America." Most emphasized, perhaps, was the argument that "in the North many of the people, ministers included, are inclined toward Modernism, Liberalism, etc. and doubt or disbelieve many of the fundamental doctrines of our faith; while we of the South are more orthodox."[60] Former Governor John M. Slaton, of Georgia, lamented that if the Southern Methodist Church merged with Northern Methodism "no more will we hear preached from its pulpit Christ and Him crucified but a conglomeration of political, sociological and interracial questions." A Methodist lay leader taunted bishops and other unionists "to tender their resignation and go."[61]

But most denominational leaders championed the cause of union with equal fervor. The Nashville *Christian Advocate* warned that any defeat of the merger plan in the southern church must be attributed to "sectional enmity and racial prejudice."[62] An Alabamian complained that "the whole

---

submitted to the presbyteries for ratification. The moderator of the southern church blamed the defeat on the 1954 Supreme Court ruling on school segregation: "This ruling gave the opposition to union an opportunity to flood the South with misinformation as to the real issue."

[59] Nashville *Christian Advocate*, July 11, 1937.

[60] *Ibid.*, July 2, Sept. 10, Oct. 8, 1937.

[61] Methodist Episcopal Church, South, General Conference, *Daily Christian Advocate* (Birmingham, Ala., 1938), Apr. 30, 1938, 7, 13.

[62] Nashville *Christian Advocate*, Sept. 3, 1937.

church cannot be hindered in its forward spiritual movement by opposition from South Carolina, Georgia and North Mississippi."[63] Bishop W. N. Ainsworth, who had opposed unification in the 1920's, now proclaimed "with profound conviction" the urgent need to unite. "There are grave problems to be solved in the nation's life," he declared, "and their nature and magnitude are such that they will not be solved by the people of the North or the people of the South or the people of the West. They will be solved by the whole people working together."[64]

Ainsworth's plea well spoke an altered tone and temper. Whereas, in 1924 and 1925, unification was endorsed in the southern church by votes of 297 to 75 in the General Conference and 4,528 to 4,108 in the annual conferences (far less than the necessary three-fourths majority), it was ratified in 1937 and 1938 by margins of 434 to 26 in the General Conference and 7,650 to 1,247 in the annual conferences. Only the North Mississippi Annual Conference held out for continued separation.[65] Moreover, the plan adopted necessitated structural adjustments of greater scope than was proposed in the 1920's. Whereas the constitution previously rejected would have joined the sectional churches as two autonomous "jurisdictions," the union consummated in 1939 provided for five geographical jurisdictions in the United States, only one of which derived mainly from the southern church. Negro conferences of the northern church were grouped into a separate and special Central Jurisdiction.[66] Though the united church

[63] Methodist Episcopal Church, South, General Conference, *Daily Christian Advocate*, Apr. 30, 1938, 20.

[64] Nashville *Christian Advocate*, Sept. 24, 1937.

[65] Methodist Episcopal Church, South, General Conference, *Journal*, 1926, 316–17; *Journal*, 1938 (Nashville, 1938), 252.

[66] The Methodist Church, *Discipline* (Nashville, 1940), *passim*. A substantial majority of the conferences in the Central Jurisdiction were located in the South. Negro congregations with approximately 7,000 members remained outside the Central Jurisdiction in predominantly white conferences in nonsouthern areas; probably less than 1,000 Negro Methodists in those areas belonged to racially integrated congregations. The aggregate of more than

was thus racially segregated, Negroes were accorded equal status in the highest councils. At quadrennial general conferences, delegates from the Central Jurisdiction sat and voted with delegates from the white jurisdictions. The original college of bishops included several Negroes. Since new bishops were to be elected by jurisdictions, Negroes would continue to be among those consecrated as the church's highest prelates.

With Methodist unification thus achieved, with Northern and Southern Presbyterians embarked on negotiations toward merger, with relations between Baptists established on a new footing of intersectional amity, it was clear that the depression decade was no ordinary interlude in the history of southern Protestantism. Church commitments to judge secular institutions and to strive for worldly betterment were more firmly and generally rooted than before, even among the Baptists. Regional characteristics faded swiftly in some congregations and slowly in others; but fade they did throughout the South.

300,000 Negroes in the Methodist Church was more than in all other predominantly white Protestant denominations in the United States combined. (Culver, *Negro Segregation in The Methodist Church,* 69, 83, 180–81.)

7

SINCE 1940

$\mathcal{T}$hrough World War II on into the perilous 1960's the tempo of change continued to quicken. There was hardly any relationship, James Reston observed—"whether of nation to nation, President to Congress, Congress to Supreme Court, labor to management, teacher to students, minister, priest, or rabbi to congregation, or even parent to child—that is not caught up in unfamiliar problems, without dependable guide lines from the past."[1] Research and technology burgeoned under the stimulus of government contracts. Production needs and economic prosperity hastened the decline of horse-drawn plows and family-sized farms. Kerosene lamps and share-crop tenancy moved rapidly from the scene. Welfare programs, the income tax, and social security mitigated extremes both in poverty and in wealth. A continuing revolution in communications outdated old concepts of time and dis-

[1] New York *Times* (Western Edition), Aug. 23, 1963.

tance. C. Vann Woodward marveled at the relentless speed
of the bulldozer as it prepared the way for metropolitan expansions, and also at "its supreme disregard for obstacles, its
heedless methods."[2] With rude, bulldozerlike abruptness, an
urban-industrial order rose to ascendance in the South, an
order keyed to progress, heedless often of the past, more
affluent, more heterogeneous than the order it supplanted.

Amidst the swirl churchmen faced baffling complexities.
For adjustments which might have been made over long in-
tervals now were compressed in a few years' span. In fashion-
oriented congregations, a subdued ritual of commitment supplanted the once vibrant experience of regeneration, albeit the
commitment itself seemed poorly comprehended. The exercise
of church discipline and strictures against worldliness had
fallen generally into disfavor. Distinctions between believers
and nonbelievers faded. Indeed one Baptist editor questioned
whether "church membership means anything in this generation." "What," he asked, "has become of the practice of
withdrawing fellowship from those who belong to the church
and work for the devil?"[3] The southern churches were surely
less identified with the status quo than they had been a generation before, and yet they had not emerged as engines of social
reconstruction. Of course spiritual needs remained to be dealt
with. Pathos and anxiety persisted; new uncertainties arose as
old ones ended.

Progress was perhaps most conspicuous in the art of public
relations. Harmony preachments seemed often to take precedence over spiritual homilies. One editor marveled that "there
wasn't the slightest sound of a discord" in the 1950 Southern
Baptist Convention.[4] But another—less elated by such displays

---

[2] Woodward, *Burden of Southern History*, 6.
[3] Macon, Georgia, *Christian Index*, Mar. 17, 1949. A brief sociological
analysis of contemporary southern Protestantism is given in Samuel Hill, Jr.,
"The South's Culture-Protestantism," *Christian Century*, LXXIX (July-Dec.
1962), 1094–96.
[4] Macon, Georgia, *Christian Index*, May 8, 1950.

of amity—fretted that church leaders now held it "a sin and a crime" to air religious controversies in the denominational press.[5] The Oklahoma *Baptist Messenger* acclaimed the suggestion of a sales executive that "the Sunday school could be sold to the public as successfully as cars, washing machines, or whatever it was that he [the salesman] had been merchandising," and the Georgia *Christian Index* rejoiced that "many tricks of the advertising trade can be adapted to the promotion of the church and its program." The Georgia journal told of one congregation that stimulated interest by designating a "man of the month," and of another that advertised on printed cards hung on door knobs.[6] One editor cited Aimee Semple McPherson as proof that "there is a big place for dramatics in our church programs, and [that] that church which can utilize, correctly [,] the dramatic elements in worship will not have to worry about lack of money or empty pews."[7] Though such notions were certainly not new, the era after World War II was singularly one of contrived appeals, of catch phrases, of canvasses, quotas, and pledges. In the churches as in secular society, drive followed drive, campaign followed campaign. Many clergymen proclaimed tithing as an obligatory commitment. "Numbers and statistical tables are the bane of Methodist organizations," a student of contemporary Methodism declares.[8]

But temporal interests were seldom broadly extended; the great challenges which preoccupied diplomats, statesmen, and social reformers still concerned many churchmen little. A typical report of the Georgia Baptist Social Service Commission in the early 1940's carried pronouncements on "Working with Soldiers," "the Growing Menace of Venereal Diseases,"

[5] Birmingham *Alabama Christian Advocate*, May 23, 1950.

[6] Oklahoma City *Baptist Messenger*, May 27, 1948; Macon, Georgia, *Christian Index*, Oct. 20, 1949.

[7] Louisville *Western Recorder*, Oct. 19, 1944.

[8] Walter G. Muelder, *Methodism and Society in the Twentieth Century* (*Methodism and Society* [4 vols., New York, 1961–62], II), 392.

and "the Liquor Traffic," but held silent on controversial economic and social issues.[9] An analysis of 447 Protestant sermons in one southern city revealed a dearth of attention to "problems of everyday living" and only a "limited amount of preaching which would help the worshiper toward a better understanding of himself, his inner urges and the methods by which they can be satisfied."[10] The *Arkansas Methodist* scolded pastors for preaching on "questions that nobody is asking."[11] Blue law enforcement, the question of diplomatic ties with the Vatican, the prospect of a return to national prohibition, and President Truman's profanity engaged the interest of some editors. In the 1940's the *Christian Index* inveighed against dance instruction at recreational centers for military servicemen, and the *Western Recorder* abhorred dancing at youth centers in Kentucky.[12] When the editor of the *Mississippi Methodist Advocate* boasted in 1950 that "the Methodist Church is the only National Protestant body which is taking a fighting stand on certain red hot issues now before us," he alluded only to prohibition and "the question of the continued separation of church and state."[13] Amidst the debate over the Presidential succession in 1944, the *Western Recorder* wondered "what Mrs. Roosevelt and other mothers of the nation have to say about the terrible growth of alcoholism among the youth of the nation since the trucks unloaded their first cargo of legal beer at the White House."[14] The *Baptist Messenger* hoped that Oklahoma's tenacious fidelity to prohibition might draw "Christian people of many states who are sick of the whiskey traffic's effrontery and start

[9] Macon, Georgia, *Christian Index*, Dec. 10, 1942.

[10] James Houston Ivey, "A Study of Preaching in Southern Churches," *Review and Expositor*, XL (Oct. 1943), 454.

[11] Little Rock *Arkansas Methodist*, June 12, 1947.

[12] Macon, Georgia, *Christian Index*, Oct. 21, Dec. 2, 1943; Louisville *Western Recorder*, Aug. 30, 1945.

[13] Jackson *Mississippi Methodist Advocate*, quoted in Little Rock *Arkansas Methodist*, Feb. 9, 1950.

[14] Louisville *Western Recorder*, June 22, 1944.

a new migration in this direction of the kind of families who built a great state here in the beginning."[15] Appalled at what he construed to be trivialities, one Alabama Methodist clergyman inquired whether "we ministers have not failed in our duty to disclose to our people in these distressing times the position of our Church in the matter of Christian social relations";[16] a Baptist theologian similarly observed that few recommendations of his denomination's social service commission had been "put into actual practice by Southern Baptists, either by the denomination, the churches, or by individuals";[17] a Southern Presbyterian committee concluded that their church lacked "a vital relation to the community life around it."[18]

Perhaps a majority of the scattered comments on economic policy which now appeared in the religious press were sympathetic toward New Deal regulatory and welfare programs. Rarely was the capitalistic system or the profit motive denigrated, however, as often they had been during the depression. A few editors were perturbed at the proliferation of governmental functions. The *Arkansas Methodist* proclaimed that "one of the greatest dangers to the progress, the greatness and even the existence of our national life is the willingness on the part of so many of our people to surrender personal initiative for government subsidy, and to depend on the government for the solution of so many of our everyday problems of life."[19] The Georgia Baptist *Christian Index* lamented that "there is not a city nor a county seat in America in which our paternal Government has not cut the muscles of self-reliance."[20] The

[15] Oklahoma City *Baptist Messenger*, Oct. 13, 1949.

[16] Birmingham *Alabama Christian Advocate*, Mar. 28, 1950.

[17] Davis C. Hill, "Southern Baptist Thought and Action in Race Relations, 1940–1950," doctoral dissertation, Southern Baptist Theological Seminary, 1952, 200.

[18] (Southern Presbyterian) *Senior Bible Studies, July-September, 1950* (Richmond, Va., 1950), 23.

[19] Little Rock *Arkansas Methodist*, Nov. 13, 1947.

[20] Macon, Georgia, *Christian Index*, Apr. 2, 1942.

Western Recorder expressed anxieties about the Tennessee Valley Authority, warning that this agency would be un-American and "terribly dangerous to any republican government" unless stringently controlled.[21] Several southern religious journals supported Senator McCarthy's investigations. "If we justify the dropping of hundreds of tons of bombs on the cities of North Korea with the inevitable destruction of many civilians and much damage of private property," the editor of the *Arkansas Methodist* reasoned, "why be so careful of the civil and social rights of Communists in America?"[22] The *Alabama Christian Advocate* grieved that "enemies of our American democracy and foes of our Christian faith and institutions are infiltrating our ranks"; the editor rejoiced that the Federal Bureau of Investigation was "alert and busy."[23]

Yet social ills received increasing scrutiny at highest denominational levels. In 1946 the Southern Presbyterian General Assembly reorganized its Permanent Committee on Social and Moral Welfare as a Department of Christian Relations. On a meager annual appropriation of only $300, the old committee had done little but draft yearly pronouncements for submission to the assembly. The new agency was provided with a full-time secretariat and with an initial budget of $20,000; it was commissioned to "produce suitable literature for informational and instructional purposes," to "speak to the churches" on social issues, and to "speak for the churches when commissioned to do so, or when the Assembly's [social] pronouncements are to be carried out."[24] The Southern Baptist Social Service Commission was similarly upgraded in 1947 when the convention increased its yearly appropriation from $1,800 to $10,000 and authorized an executive secretary to

[21] Louisville *Western Recorder*, June 1, 1944.
[22] Little Rock *Arkansas Methodist*, Sept. 7, 1950.
[23] Birmingham *Alabama Christian Advocate*, July 18, 1950.
[24] Presbyterian Church in the United States, General Assembly, *Minutes, 1946* (Richmond, Va., 1946), 166–68.

direct it; redesignated as a Christian Life Commission in 1953, the agency later received supplementary support from the Ford Foundation.[25] Through published pamphlets and tracts, study conferences, and by various other means, the commission strove to inculcate Christian attitudes. Occasionally its viewpoints were reflected in the denominational Sunday school literature; for example, one lesson in 1950 belittled Christians who "do not feel any responsibility whatsoever toward the cancerous conditions of a corrupting social order about them."[26] And the Methodist Church established a Board of Social and Economic Relations in 1952 to promote the denominational social creed, "to make available to the Church membership resource material relating to the field of social and economic relations, to respond to requests of local church groups for information and guidance; to encourage and stimulate interest and activity in the relation of the program of the Church to social and economic problems. . . ."[27]

Of all problems in the social order, race relations was the one problem which most unsettled—and indeed imperiled—the southern churches. For a complex of technological, moral, economic, and political forces—forces long at work—moved rapidly now to undermine old traditions of white supremacy. The ruthless persecution of Jews in Europe tended to infamize racial and ethnic discriminations everywhere; mass education presumably reduced old prejudices. Denominational boards devoted major efforts to advancing racial justice in the 1940's and afterward, as did a few religious newspapers. "Until we break down racial prejudices within the boundaries of our own

[25] Interview with the Reverend A. C. Miller, Executive Secretary of the Southern Baptist Christian Life Commission, July 21, 1955; Hill, "Southern Baptist Thought and Action in Race Relations, 1940–1950," 200.

[26] (Southern Baptist Sunday School Board) *The Teacher, July 1950* (Nashville, 1950), 3.

[27] The Methodist Church, General Conference, *Journal, 1952* (Nashville, 1952), 1420. The General Conference of 1960 merged the Board of Social and Economic Relations with the Boards of Peace and Temperance to form the Board of Christian Social Concerns.

land and prove by its working that a program of racial adjustment is practical," declared the Kentucky Baptist *Western
Recorder* in 1942, "we shall be heard with little serious attention when we speak about removing the larger and far more
complicated racial antipathies and antagonisms which the
would-be dictators of the world are using today for their own
advancements. . . ."[28] A lesson in the Southern Presbyterian
Sunday school literature in 1950 stressed that there was no
divine warrant for racial segregation; another essay contrasted
"the attitude of our church today toward fellowship across
racial, national, and class lines with that given by God to his
Church."[29] A Southern Baptist Sunday school leaflet for 1950
reminded students that "race relations is a vital question to
Christians in every land" and that "you should determine
your racial attitudes in terms of Peter's vision and of his experience with Cornelius."[30] Few laymen in the lower South
seemed moved by such preachments, though like others they
fought the nation's wars extolling the cause of freedom. But
denominational leaders and rank-and-file clergymen were far
more sensitive to contradictions between principles professed
and practices condoned.

Southern Methodists abandoned all-white denomination-
ism when they merged with the northern Methodists in 1939.
The Negro minority in the united church was assigned to a
separate Central Jurisdiction. But bishops of the Central Jurisdiction exercised the same prerogatives as white bishops; black
and white delegates mingled freely at quadrennial General
Conferences; racial prejudice became a favorite subject of
analysis at church-sponsored study conferences; preachments
on the equality of men appeared often in the Sunday school

[28] Louisville *Western Recorder*, Dec. 10, 1942.
[29] (Southern Presbyterian) *Senior Bible Studies, October–December, 1950*
(Richmond, Va., 1950), 14; (Southern Presbyterian) *Senior Teacher's Guide,
October–December, 1950* (Richmond, Va., 1950), 35.
[30] (Southern Baptist Sunday School Board) *Sunday School Young People,
First Quarter, 1950* (Nashville, 1950), 15.

literature. A committee of the Fairfield, Alabama, Methodist Church voiced a general complaint in 1950 when it protested that denominational publications propounded the "non-segregation of the races, and a way of life contrary to the tradition and best interest of our society." The North Alabama Annual Conference grumbled about a "sectional" (i.e., pronorthern) prejudice in the church.[31] Such protests availed little. An official of the denominational board of education challenged one disgruntled group to "send me immediately any quotations, giving name of publication, date of issue and page number, which you feel are contrary to the teachings of Jesus Christ and to the position of The Methodist Church."[32] Proclaiming that there was "no place in The Methodist Church for racial discrimination or racial segregation," the quadrennial General Conference of 1952 pledged to work to rid the denomination of these evils.[33] Yet the continuation of the Central Jurisdiction showed that much remained to be accomplished.

Similar tendencies were likewise manifest in the still-sectional Southern Presbyterian and Southern Baptist denominations. Hence in 1947 the Southern Presbyterian General Assembly exhorted church members to align themselves with "those forces that seek to uphold for all kinds and classes of Americans their civil and constitutional liberties."[34] And in 1949 it passed on to local congregations for their "consideration and study" a fourteen-page report on "States' Rights and Human Rights." The document urged rank-and-file members not to abdicate their responsibilities for racial adjustments to "secular, non-Protestant, and non-Southern Christian forces"; it admonished ministers not to be "guilty of supporting by

[31] Birmingham *Alabama Christian Advocate*, May 2, Nov. 11, 1950.

[32] An initialed carbon of the letter containing the challenge is in the files of the author.

[33] The Methodist Church, General Conference, *Journal, 1952*, 1417.

[34] Presbyterian Church in the United States, General Assembly, *Minutes, 1947*, 165.

their silence an unchristian social order"; the need for civil rights legislation was implied.[35] A Negro delegate was appointed chairman of a standing committee in the assembly of 1942; but, owing to objections raised by other delegates, he did not personally render his report as chairmen customarily did. Heeding the strong protests of several presbyteries, the assembly the next year formally apologized, and directed that henceforth "every commissioner [delegate] regardless of race or color be accorded the full rights and privileges of the Assembly." The assembly of 1944 took pains to correct one statement prepared for its adoption "by the capitalization of the initial letter of the word 'Negro' in the report."[36] Accommodations at the church-owned assembly grounds at Montreat, North Carolina, were desegregated early in the 1950's (until then Negroes attending official functions there had been fed separately and housed in accommodations normally assigned to custodians). Steps were also taken to integrate constituent jurisdictions of the church. The all-Negro Snedecor Memorial Synod was abolished in 1951 and its presbyteries reassigned to predominantly white synods on the basis of geographical location;[37] some Negro presbyteries subsequently merged with white presbyteries. A very few Negro congregations remained in predominantly white presbyteries to which they had belonged over the years. The almost all-white Brazos Presbytery, in southeastern Texas, chose one of its two Negro clergymen as moderator in 1956.[38]

The Southern Baptist Convention took an historic step in 1946 when it designated a special committee to draft a race

[35] Presbyterian Church in the United States, General Assembly, *Minutes, 1949* (Richmond, Va., 1949), 191.

[36] Presbyterian Church in the United States, General Assembly, *Minutes, 1943* (Richmond, Va., 1943), 74; *Minutes, 1944* (Richmond, Va., 1944), 83.

[37] Presbyterian Church in the United States, General Assembly, *Minutes, 1951* (Richmond, Va., 1951), 84. In 1946 there were only 3,368 Negro members of the Southern Presbyterian Church. All but eight Negro congregations were at that time assigned to the Snedecor Memorial Synod. (Presbyterian Church in the United States, General Assembly, *Minutes, 1946*, 137.)

[38] New York *Times*, Jan. 29, 1956.

relations pronouncement. In ratifying the committee's "Statement of Principles" the next year, the convention acknowledged its responsibility "for the promotion of inter-racial good-will" and urged "upon our Baptist people and all Christians the duty of ordering our racial attitudes and actions in accordance with Christian truth and Christian love." Delegates pledged specifically that:

1. We shall think of the Negro as a person and treat him accordingly.
2. We shall continually strive as individuals to conquer all prejudice and eliminate from our speech terms of contempt and from our conduct actions of ill will.
3. We shall teach our children that prejudice is un-Christian and that good-will and helpful deeds are the duty of every Christian toward all men of all races.
4. We shall protest against injustice and indignities against Negroes, as we do in the case of people of our own race, whenever and wherever we meet them.
5. We shall be willing for the Negro to enjoy the rights granted to him under the Constitution of the United States, including the right to vote, to serve on juries, to receive justice in the courts, to be free from mob violence, to secure a just share of the benefits of educational and other funds and to receive equal service for equal payment on public carriers and conveniences.
6. We shall be just in our dealing with the Negro as an individual. Whenever he is in our employ we shall pay him an adequate wage and provide for him healthful working conditions.
7. We shall strive to promote community good-will between the races in every way possible.
8. We shall actively co-operate with Negro Baptists in the building up of their churches, the education of their ministers, and the promotion of their missions and evangelistic programs.

The convention went on to endorse a long-range educational

program in race relations—through pastoral sermons, through pamphlets, study courses, and other literature prepared by convention agencies, through articles and editorials contributed to state Baptist papers, through race relations courses at denominational colleges, and through co-operation between Negro and white Baptist leaders at the community level.[39]

Several state Baptist organizations acted along parallel lines.[40] The 1946 North Carolina State Baptist Convention at first resolved that "segregation of believers holding the same tenets of faith because of color or social status into racial or class churches is a denial of the New Testament affirmation of the equality of all believers"—but this resolution was rescinded before the convention adjourned. In another statement which was not rescinded, the Carolinians advocated "equal wages and equal treatment of Negro, Chinese, Japanese, and Indian employees."[41] The Georgia State Baptist Convention that year abhorred recent lynchings and exhorted white Baptists to work for "the more abundant spiritual, educational, economic and civic life" for all races.[42] The Baptist General Association of Virginia pledged to strive "for better health, educational, and working conditions" for Negroes.[43] Actions did not always follow resolutions, though occasional gestures of accommodation were to be noted. The white Georgia state convention broke precedent in 1946 when it assembled in joint (but segregated) session with its Negro counterpart.[44] At Ridgecrest, North Carolina, in 1946, delegates of the white Baptist Student Union formally requested that Negro Baptist students be

[39] Southern Baptist Convention, *Annual, 1947* (Nashville, 1947), 47, 342–43.

[40] See Walter Spearman, "Southern Baptists Act on Race Problem," in Chapel Hill, North Carolina, *Christian Frontier*, Jan. 1947.

[41] Baptist State Convention of North Carolina, *Annual, 1946* (n.p., n.d.), 50, 92.

[42] Baptist Convention of the State of Georgia, *Minutes, 1946* (Atlanta, n.d.), 36.

[43] Baptist General Association of Virginia, *Journal, 1946* (Richmond, 1947), 85.

[44] Macon, Georgia, *Christian Index*, Nov. 28, 1946.

represented at their next annual encampment (but the petition was refused by the Southern Baptist Sunday School Board which held jurisdiction over the assembly grounds). In April 1951 the Southern Baptist theological seminaries at Louisville, New Orleans, and Fort Worth announced that henceforth they would admit all qualified applicants without distinction as to race. And Wayland Baptist College, at Plainview, Texas, became the first white Baptist college in the South to enroll a Negro, in June 1951.[45]

When the Supreme Court rendered its epochal decision on public school segregation in 1954, virtually all general denominational convocations acclaimed it. The 1956 General Conference of the Methodist Church admonished Methodists to assist in effecting the necessary adjustments "in all good faith, with brotherliness and patience"; the conference took this occasion to beg that "discrimination or segregation by any method or practice, whether by conference structure or otherwise in The Methodist Church, be abolished with reasonable speed."[46] The Southern Presbyterian General Assembly of 1954 implored "all our people to lend their assistance to those charged with the duty of implementing the decision, and to remember that appeals to racial prejudice will not help but hinder the accomplishment of this aim"; the assembly declared enforced segregation to be "out of harmony with Christian theology and ethics" and asked local congregations and church colleges to open their doors to all races.[47] The General Assembly of 1957 issued a sweeping indictment of racial discrimination in employment and politics as well as in religion and education.[48] The Southern Baptist Convention of 1954 acknowl-

[45] Hill, "Southern Baptist Thought and Action in Race Relations, 1940–1950," 328, 359, 373.

[46] The Methodist Church, General Conference, Journal, 1956 (Nashville, n.d.), 1693.

[47] Presbyterian Church in the United States, General Assembly, Minutes, 1954 (n.p., n.d.), 193, 197.

[48] Presbyterian Church in the United States, General Assembly, Minutes, 1957 (n.p., n.d.), 191–96.

edged that "this Supreme Court decision is in harmony with the constitutional guarantee of equal freedom to all citizens, and with the Christian principles of equal justice and love for all men"; it exhorted Baptists "to conduct themselves in this period of adjustment in the spirit of Christ," to give "a good testimony to the meaning of Christian faith and discipleship."[49] Amidst mounting racial strife two years later, twenty-eight Southern Baptist leaders issued an extraordinary "Appeal for a Christian Spirit in Race Relations"; among the appellants were the president of the Southern Baptist Convention, the presidents of seven Southern Baptist colleges and theological seminaries, and the heads of several convention executive agencies. They begged rank-and-file communicants to join them in seeking "new insights as to our Christian duty" and "more grace in manifesting Christian love toward all men." They affirmed their personal convictions that "every man possesses infinite worth and should be treated with respect as a person," that "the Christian view of man, every man, must reflect the spirit of the cross," and that "prejudice against persons or mistreatment of persons on the grounds of race is contrary to the will of God." They emphasized that Baptists, as the largest religious group in the South, bore heavy responsibilities for finding "a Christian solution" to the crisis.[50]

A few state and district convocations also reacted favorably to the court ruling. The Southern Presbyterian Synods of Virginia and Arkansas joined the General Assembly in applauding the Supreme Court and in condemning enforced segregation as "out of harmony with Christian theology and ethics."[51] The North Carolina Methodist Annual Conference acclaimed the ruling as a "true interpretation of our Christian faith and our American democracy"; endorsements also came from the Little Rock, North Arkansas, and North Texas

---

[49] Southern Baptist Convention, *Annual, 1954* (Nashville, 1954), 87.

[50] Nashville *Baptist and Reflector*, Apr. 12, 1956.

[51] Nashville *Southern School News*, Oct., 1954, June 1958. The Arkansas Synod reaffirmed its position in 1955, 1956, 1957, and 1958.

Methodist Annual Conferences.[52] The Baptist General Association of Virginia acknowledged "the fact that, regardless of our own personal views, the decision of the United States Supreme Court declaring segregation of races in our public schools to be unconstitutional is the supreme law of the land which does not violate any cardinal principle of our religion, and [that] as Christian citizens we should abide by this law."[53] The North Carolina State Baptist Convention resolved that "the Christian citizen of the South, if the spirit of the Court's decision is taken seriously, must re-affirm *their* [sic] *belief and teaching about man as having infinite worth in the sight of God*"; the convention requested the colleges which it supported to admit qualified Negroes.[54] When die-hard segregationists demanded that schools be closed if necessary to avert integration, the Virginia, North Georgia, South Carolina, and Florida Methodist Annual Conferences adopted resolutions calling for a continuation of public education, as did the Georgia State Baptist Convention.[55] The Texas Baptist General Convention admonished church people not to let "demogogues or radicals rob us as Christians of that moral leadership which God wants us to exert in the solution of this problem which is primarily moral and spiritual."[56] Most remarkable perhaps was the early reaction of the Baptist press. The *Arkansas Baptist* praised the pronouncement of the Southern Baptist Convention as "a fair and conservative statement on that question";[57] the North Carolina *Biblical Recorder* commended it as "a wholesome thing";[58] the Tennessee *Baptist and Re-*

[52] *Ibid.*, Dec. 1954, July 1955, July 1961, July 1962.

[53] Baptist General Association of Virginia, *Journal, 1954* (Richmond, n.d.), 88.

[54] Baptist State Convention of North Carolina, *Annual, 1954* (n.p., n.d.), 57.

[55] Nashville *Southern School News*, July 1960, Dec. 1960, July 1961, July 1962.

[56] *Ibid.*, Nov. 1954.

[57] Little Rock *Arkansas Baptist*, June 17, 1954.

[58] Raleigh *Biblical Recorder*, June 26, 1954.

flector declared that "the Convention could do no less than this";[59] and the *Alabama Baptist* believed the convention had "pointed clearly to the thinking of Southern Baptists on the Supreme Court decision." In what surely proved to be a sanguine analysis, the Alabama paper declared that "Southern Baptists are not willing to become rebels again, but to work [*sic*] along quietly and sympathetically to carry out the Supreme Court decision in a manner that will result in happiness and peace among the people."[60]

Yet, as in other matters, the appraisals and importunities of religious editors and high denominational councils were not automatically recited in local congregations. Nor did they receive automatic endorsements at intermediate ecclesiastical jurisdictions. Indeed in the years after 1954 the cleavage between rank-and-file communicants and denominational leaders widened markedly. Some pulpit preachers virtually eschewed all discussion of race and other controversial issues; the social views of some differed little from those of their congregations; most were guarded and discreet in their utterances. Nevertheless the popular disapprobation which came to center on denominational spokesmen, seminary professors, and editors of Sunday school publications projected often to clergymen collectively. Professionalization and theological training set the clergy apart as earlier unlettered preachers had not been set apart. Whereas most laymen held still to regional perspectives, pastors showed increasing detachment from the cultural milieu in which they labored, and increasingly concerned themselves with truths applicable to all men in all conditions. In many localities laymen now rallied to the defense of regional traditions as passionately as their forbears a century before. The pattern was mixed, but this was especially the case in the lower South.

Nor was the disaffection repressed or concealed. By unani-

---

[59] Nashville *Baptist and Reflector*, June 17, 1954.
[60] Birmingham *Alabama Baptist*, June 17, 1954.

mous vote of its members, the Grenada, Mississippi, First Baptist Church advised the Southern Baptist Convention that it was "not in accord with the Convention endorsement of the recent 'Supreme Court decision on segregation in public education.' " The Mississippians threatened to secede from the convention if pronouncements of this nature continued; they also expressed their opposition to "anything that smacks of socialism, modernism, or communism; or any other resolutions that may cause strife. . . ."[61] The Presbyterian Synod of Mississippi advised the General Assembly that it could not "in good conscience comply with the recommendations with respect to institutions under its control or to the various conferences sponsored by the Synod, nor can it place the stamp of its approval upon the recommendation that sessions of constituent churches of this Synod admit persons to membership and fellowship without reference to race."[62] By margin of more than three to one, the Georgia State Baptist Convention rejected a resolution which would have aligned it with the Southern Baptist Convention in supporting the Supreme Court decision.[63] A group of Mississippi Methodists banded together in 1957 to agitate against the "repeated presentation of the topic of integration in the church literature"; they announced that many Mississippi Methodist congregations had stopped using the official church literature "largely because of the contribution of such articles and matters of similar nature therein."[64] A prominent Louisiana Baptist layman, F. C. Haley, superintendent of the Claiborne Parish public schools, warned in 1959 that if the Southern Baptist Convention "does not cease its sinister maneuvers against Southern traditions, we can repeal them at the local level by being less cooperative with their cooperative program." He particularly deplored the propensity of clergymen "to meddle in fields

---

[61] Jackson *Baptist Record*, June 10, 1954.
[62] Nashville *Southern School News*, Dec. 1954.
[63] *Ibid.*, Dec. 1956.
[64] *Ibid.*, Oct. 1957.

for which they are not educationally or temperamentally equipped."[65] Contrary to principles enunciated by high prelates and councils, hundreds of white congregations turned away Negroes seeking admittance to their services.

Southern Protestant schools clung to segregated patterns more tenaciously than public institutions. Though 105 of 206 state colleges and universities in the South were desegregated by 1957, as were 35 of 45 such Catholic schools, only 55 of 188 Protestant institutions of higher learning in the area were at that time biracial.[66] Not until 1961 were Negroes admitted into any of the seven colleges and junior colleges operated by the white North Carolina State Baptist Convention. At that time the four colleges operated by the Tennessee State Baptist Convention remained all-white, and Wayland remained the only Southern Baptist college in Texas which had accepted Negroes.[67] Trustees of Methodist-sponsored Hendrix College, at Conway, Arkansas, rejected an integration proposal in 1960. Two years earlier Mississippi Methodists were explicitly reassured that "segregation always has been, and is now, the policy of Millsaps College. There is no thought, purpose or intention on the part of those in charge of its affairs to change this policy"; the controlling board which issued this statement was headed by Bishop Marvin Franklin.[68] Amidst a fund-raising campaign for two new Methodist colleges in North Carolina, in 1958, the chairman of the annual conference board of education promised that there were "no plans for integration in any shape, form, or fashion" at these campuses.[69] Wake Forest, Davidson, Duke, Meredith, and Southern

[65] Shreveport *Times*, June 10, 1959.

[66] Nashville *Southern School News*, Mar. 1957.

[67] *Ibid.*, April, Dec. 1961.

[68] *Ibid.*, April 1958, June 1961. The Hendrix action is well treated in Robert Paul Sessions, "Are Southern Ministers Failing the South?" *Saturday Evening Post*, CCXXXIV, May 13, 1961, 37, 82–83, 85, 88. Sessions concluded that "it now appears that two sectarian schools, Hendrix and Ouachita Baptist College, may be the last strongholds of segregation among the Arkansas colleges. . . ." But both schools have since acted to desegregate.

[69] Nashville *Southern School News*, Dec. 1958.

Methodist University first admitted Negroes to their undergraduate colleges in 1962; not until the autumn of 1963 did Baylor University Trustees vote to admit qualified Negroes.[70] Fourteen of twenty-three Southern Presbyterian junior and senior colleges remained racially unmixed in May 1963.[71]

In analyzing a serious racial crisis at Cambridge, Maryland, in 1963, one journalist surmised that, though political, social, and moral considerations all "figured in the controversy's resolution," "the effective pressure to end the crisis came from within the business community." He believed that this was true also at Little Rock, Birmingham, Atlanta, and numerous other localities where similar crises erupted. Hence he concluded that "economic self-interest frequently leads to racial change in situations where other factors seemingly have little influence."[72] Events over a previous period of years seemed amply to verify his conclusion. Of course businessmen shared leadership with various action groups, with the courts, with local school and law enforcement officials, and sometimes with the United States Army. But the over-all role of the clergy was clearly secondary. Nor was this altogether for lack of effort. Thus, as Dallas prepared for school desegregation in 1958, 300 local white Protestant clergymen jointly proclaimed that "enforced segregation is morally and legally wrong," and implored all citizens to co-operate in making the required adjustments.[73] In similar circumstances that same year, 311 Atlanta ministers and rabbis appealed for law obedience, for the preservation of public schools, and for tolerance of differences of opinion.[74] A group of Little Rock churchmen, including an Episcopalian bishop, a Methodist bishop, and the president of the local ministerial association, urged the reopening of schools which had been closed in that city to avert

[70] *Ibid.*, Oct. 1962, May 1963; El Paso *Herald-Post*, Nov. 2, 1963.
[71] Nashville *Southern School News*, May 1963.
[72] Claude Sitton in New York *Times* (Western Edition), July 29, 1963.
[73] Dallas *Morning News*, Apr. 27, 28, 1958.
[74] Baton Rouge *Morning Advocate*, Nov. 23, 1958.

integration.[75] The Richmond Ministers' Association published a fifteen-hundred word "statement of conviction on race" early in 1957 which criticized the Virginia governor for "exceedingly inept handling of the current racial situation." And 125 ministers and rabbis of Greater Miami released a statement early in 1959 urging the continuation of public education and deploring all "hatred and scorn for those of another race."[76] So it was in city after city.

Such appeals were weakened by clerical disclaimers, however, and by hostile responses from religious lay leaders. The plea of the 300 antisegregationist clergymen in Dallas brought forth a rejoinder from 330 preachers who inveighed with equal fervor against "enforced integration."[77] The 311 Atlanta clergymen who urged compliance were answered by 53 others who held racial integration to be "Satanic, unconstitutional and one of the main objectives of the Communist Party. . . ."[78] Governor Faubus was not without clerical allies at Little Rock; indeed a key official in the racist Capital Citizens Council was the Reverend Wesley Pruden, pastor of the Broadmoor Baptist Church.[79] In the autumn of 1962 officials of the Rosedale, Mississippi, Presbyterian Church refused to permit the reading to the congregation of a presbyterial letter dealing with the crisis at the University of Mississippi. A spokesman explained that "the Session felt that the letter was an attempt in the name of Christianity to implant in the minds of the people a sense of guilt and shame, when actually any guilt and shame should be felt by the Administration in Washington and not the people of Mississippi."[80] Clergymen who advocated moderation often met crude reprisals. Outraged white supremacists physically assaulted a Clinton, Tennessee, Bap-

[75] *Ibid.*, Sept. 28, 1958.
[76] Nashville *Southern School News*, Feb. 1957, Mar. 1959.
[77] Dallas *Morning News*, May 18, 1958.
[78] Nashville *Southern School News*, Apr. 1959.
[79] Baton Rouge *Morning Advocate*, Sept. 28, 1958.
[80] Memphis *Commercial Appeal*, Oct. 25, 1962.

tist clergyman in 1956 when he escorted six Negro students to a newly integrated school.[81] The Sumter County, Georgia, Ministerial Association was censured by a local grand jury in 1956 for a resolution which it adopted deploring acts of violence against the racially integrated Koinonia Farm Incorporated. Jurors blamed the eccentric inhabitants of the farm for the disturbances and exonerated the surrounding community. And they advised the preachers that "the people of this county are entitled to expect the sincere cooperation and helpfulness of those gentlemen who constitute the personnel of the Ministerial Association. If they are going to live with us they should work with us, and if they can't do us good, they should strive not to do us harm."[82] An Alabama Methodist layman curtly advised preachers who disliked the South's racial mores that there were "well paved roads in reach for automobiles —and even for attached trailers carrying household goods— leading to the north."[83] Some pastors lost their pulpits. By congregational vote the Reverend Cecil Robert Taylor was summarily discharged as minister of the Danville, Virginia, First Christian Church, in 1963; the move came after Taylor and twelve other local ministers begged that Negroes be included on the mayor's racial advisory committee.[84] At Columbus, Georgia, in 1959, the Reverend Robert B. McNeill was dismissed from his pulpit at the First Presbyterian Church after advocating interracial contacts between white and Negro leaders in an article published in *Look* magazine; the action was by a special judicial commission of the Southwest Georgia Presbytery which had been appointed to investigate complaints of unrest in the congregation.[85] In June 1963, five months after twenty-eight Mississippi Methodist clergymen

---

[81] Nashville *Southern School News*, Jan. 1957.
[82] *Race Relations Law Reporter*, II (June 1957), 688.
[83] Birmingham *Alabama Christian Advocate*, Apr. 4, 1950.
[84] Danville *Bee*, Aug. 5, 1963; Danville *Register*, Aug. 6, 1963.
[85] Baton Rouge *State-Times*, June 9, 1959. See Robert B. McNeill, "A Georgia Minister Offers a Solution for the South," *Look*, May 21, 1957, 55–58, 63–64.

issued a manifesto opposing racial discrimination and pleading for the freedom of ministers to speak their convictions, only nine of the twenty-eight remained with the congregations they served when the document was published. Twelve had departed from the state and seven had been moved to other pastorates in Mississippi. Congregational and community pressures—including acts of vandalism and intimidation—seemed to account for most of the transfers.[86] At his own request the Reverend W. B. Selah was relieved of his pastorate at the Jackson, Mississippi, Galloway Methodist Church, largest Methodist congregation in the state. Selah sought another assignment when lay officials ignored his importunities and turned away Negroes from a worship service.[87] Moral leadership seemed woefully inadequate where opinion was so rigidly fixed, where expression of divergent viewpoints was so little tolerated, and where forces of repression were so organized and aroused.

But of course the churches did not survive in a context of race relations alone. A multitude of traditional functions remained to be discharged. Under the auspices of the churches the gospel was yet proclaimed, converts baptized, the Lord's Supper administered, marriages solemnized, the sick, infirm, and bereaved comforted, the rites of burial recited over the dead. Though revivals waned in Methodist and Presbyterian congregations, among Baptists they flourished still. Nor were the vital social accompaniments of religious participation a thing of the past. Opportunities for fellowship ranged from ladies' circle meetings, to men's suppers, to informal "family-night" gatherings. Young people were attracted by church-sponsored sporting and recreational events as well as by youth-oriented religious exercises; dating and mating evolved often under the purview of the church. Over the South hundreds of humanitarian and educational institutions remained

[86] New York *Times* (Western Edition), Jan. 19, June 29, 1963.
[87] Memphis *Commercial Appeal*, Aug. 12, 1963.

under church sponsorship—including hospitals, orphanages, homes for the aged, colleges, universities, theological seminaries, research repositories, and publication establishments. And the southern churches maintained their heavy support of missions in foreign fields.

The spectacular growth of the Southern Baptists was one of the more conspicuous trends in American Protestantism in the post-World War II era. "It is a fact," noted the editor of the Dallas *Baptist Standard* in 1949, "that Baptists have gained more rapidly in the past 10 years than in any single decade in our history. This is true throughout the Southern Baptist Convention, and especially here in Texas."[88] In twenty-seven white annual conferences of the Methodist Church in the South, membership grew from 2,837,262 in 1940 to 4,046,534 in 1962; membership in the (Southern) Presbyterian Church in the United States rose from 449,045 in 1936 to 928,055 in 1962. But aggregate membership of congregations affiliated with the Southern Baptist Convention burgeoned from 2,700,155 in 1936 to 10,191,303 in 1962.[89]

Many factors helped account for the Baptist upsurge. Of course Baptist leaders relied heavily on studied promotional techniques as did leaders of other religious groups. Moreover, their programs and appeals could be tempered to the predilections of each locality to a degree seldom possible in rival communions—particularly those organized under coercive

[88] Dallas *Baptist Standard*, quoted in Birmingham *Alabama Christian Advocate*, July 12, 1949.

[89] US Department of Commerce, Bureau of the Census, *Religious Bodies: 1936* (3 vols., Washington, D. C., 1941), I, 374–423, 870–99; *Yearbook of American Churches, 1964*, ed. Benson Y. Landis (New York, 1964), 254, 258. The Methodist statistics are for annual conferences located in the South and assigned to the Southeastern and South Central jurisdictions; they are taken from the *General Minutes of the Annual Conferences of The Methodist Church, 1962* (Nashville, 1962), 753, 782, and *General Minutes of the Annual Conferences of The Methodist Church, 1940* (Nashville, 1941), 272, 278. Though the Southern Baptists increased in some areas in the North and West, their main growth was in the South. Another conservatively oriented, congregationally autonomous group—the Churches of Christ—experienced a similar rapid growth in some southern localities.

hierarchies. It was generally understood that the pronouncements of Baptist associations and conventions spoke only for the delegates who voted them, that no position was binding on a Baptist congregation unless adopted by the congregation itself, that Baptists ordained, employed, controlled, and discharged clergymen with a freedom denied Methodists and Presbyterians. The congregation itself was a court of highest appeal on matters of faith, morals, admission, and expulsion. Hence, early in 1962, the Oklahoma City First Baptist Church voted 327 to 311 to deny membership to a Negro who asked to join.[90] On the other hand, a survey in 1963 revealed that at least 234 Southern Baptist congregations in Texas had adopted policies of receiving Negroes into membership on the same basis as whites; presumably some others would accept Negroes if they desired to affiliate.[91] Exercising their freedom of action, two Southern Baptist associations in Texas and New Mexico admitted several all-Negro congregations in the middle 1950's (and hence brought them into affiliation with the Southern Baptist Convention).[92] The Southern Baptist General Convention of Texas duly received and accredited Negro delegates from Austin and Corpus Christi in 1961.[93]

Doctrinal conservatism was a great fountain of Baptist unity and strength. Southern Baptists wavered markedly in their aversions to worldly pleasures, to conspicuous affluence, and to urban social conformity. But through change and upheaval, amidst new modes and outlooks, they clung steadfastly to religious concepts of the past. One Baptist preacher was "more tremendously convinced than ever [in 1949] that the last hope,

[90] Nashville *Baptist and Reflector, Jan. 18, 1962.*

[91] Dallas *Morning News,* Sept. 19, 1963. This was the finding of the public relations department of the Baptist General Convention of Texas, which sent questionnaires to 4,000 congregations; 1,259 congregations responded.

[92] Postal card from Austin, Texas, Baptist Association to Department of Survey, Statistics, and Information, Southern Baptist Sunday School Board, dated Nov. 18, 1955 (in the files of the Department of Survey, Statistics, and Information); Central Baptist Association of New Mexico, *Minutes, 1955* (Albuquerque, 1955), 38.

[93] Nashville *Southern School News,* Dec. 1961.

the fairest hope, the only hope for evangelizing this world on New Testament principles is the Southern Baptist people represented in that [Southern Baptist] Convention. I mean no unkindness to anybody on earth but if you call that bigotry then make the most of it."[94] His view was pridefully shared by many of his co-religionists, and indeed (less pridefully) by a significant body of non-Baptists. A Methodist layman opined in 1947 that only "when our church comes back to preaching the crucified Christ as the only hope of the world, and a burning hell as the home of all who reject this Christ, and make sin horrible and tragic, take the emphasis off of theology and put it on kneeology" would it "go forward in its Holy Mission." Another lamented that "regeneration, the witness of the Spirit and the Christians [sic] growth in Grace are subjects that are never preached upon" in Methodist churches.[95] Eschewing neo-orthodoxy and ecumenism, little distracted by the insights of modern psychology and sociology, most Baptist preachers largely confined their homilies to the traditional gospel of spiritual redemption. Few hesitated to proclaim the Bible as God's literally inerrant word. The vibrant exhortations of that most renowned of all Southern Baptists—Billy Graham—belonged as much to the nineteenth as to the twentieth century. A former president of the Southern Baptist Convention, the Reverend Robert G. Lee, vividly portrayed the heavenly estate in a sermon at Louisville in 1956. He expected to sing and preach when he reached this eternal rest-

[94] Birmingham *Alabama Christian Advocate*, June 29, 1948. Louie D. Newton, *Why I Am a Baptist* (New York, 1957), includes excellent statements of prominent contemporary Southern Baptists, particularly pages 211–306. An unusually perceptive analysis of Southern Baptist attitudes is given in Samuel Hill, Jr., "The Southern Baptists: Need for Reformulation, Redirection," *Christian Century*, LXXX (Jan.–June 1963), 39–42. A liberal Southern Baptist, Hill is chairman of the Department of Religion in the University of North Carolina.

[95] Birmingham *Alabama Christian Advocate*, Sept. 11, Oct. 16, 1947. The growing contrasts between Methodists and Baptists in the South are ably discussed in George Harmon, "How to Tell a Baptist from a Methodist in the South," *Harper's Magazine*, CCXXVI, Feb. 1963, 58–63.

ing place, removed at last from such terrestrial aberrations as
toil, drunkards, grave diggers, and cemeteries. To Isaiah, Paul,
Peter, and other Biblical figures, he would say: "All you guys
—that's the way we'll talk in Heaven—I've been studying you
all my life; now you sit down and listen to me for a while."[96]
When Lee addressed the annual Texas Baptist Evangelism
Conference early in 1962 "there was hardly a dry eye" in the
auditorium where the session was held; "more than a hundred
persons with tears streaming down their cheeks walked down
the aisles to ask God to bring revivals to their lives and their
churches."[97] Accounts of revival meetings remained a conspicuous feature in most Southern Baptist papers.

Militantly oriented elements dramatically proved their
strength in the Southern Baptist Convention early in the
1960's, much as they had seventy years before during the
Whitsitt-Landmark controversy, and during the subsequent
debates over modernism in the 1920's. As in the Toy and
Whitsitt episodes, the crisis centered around the scholarly
findings of a seminarian—Professor Ralph Elliott of the Midwestern Baptist Theological Seminary, in Kansas City, whose
The Message of Genesis was published in the summer of
1961. Elliott's interpretations of creation, Adam, and the flood
appeared cautious and conservative by ordinary standards, but
the Southern Baptist standards were not ordinary. A significant body of Southern Baptists still regarded virtually all
modern Biblical scholarship with distrust. The Kansas *Baptist
Digest* feared that "if we accept this book, our theological
students will come out of our seminaries more and more
liberal as the years go by" and "we will take our place with
others that God has put on the shelf."[98] No doubt this apprehension was widely shared.

The seminary board of trustees at first supported the young

[96] Louisville *Courier Journal*, Jan. 19, 1956.
[97] Kansas City *Word and Way*, Mar. 8, 1962.
[98] Quoted *ibid.*, Jan. 11, 1962.

author. Following a special meeting in December 1961, it was announced that "while there are members of the Board of Trustees who are in disagreement with some of the interpretations presented by Dr. Elliott in his book, we do affirm our confidence in him as a consecrated Christian, a promising scholar and teacher, a loyal servant of Southern Baptists, and a dedicated and warmly evangelistic preacher of the Gospel."[99] A few weeks later the Southern Baptist Sunday School Board vigorously defended the action of its Broadman Press in publishing the work. "In accepting the book for publication," declared the Sunday School Board in a formal statement,

Broadman Press recognized that the point of view expressed in the book would not be coincident with the thinking of all Baptists. It was considered, however, to be representative of a segment of Southern Baptist life and thought. . . . Broadman Press ministers to the denomination in keeping with the historic Baptist principle of the freedom of the individual to interpret the Bible for himself, to hold a particular theory of inspiration of the Bible which seems most reasonable to him, and to develop his beliefs in accordance with his theory.[100]

But such pleas and assurances did not quieten the storm. In making known his displeasure with the seminary trustees, the editor of the Kansas City (Southern Baptist) *Word and Way* took pains to point out that "editorials and articles which have appeared since the board's meeting in state Baptist papers in Texas, Oklahoma, Mississippi, Illinois, Kansas, and Tennessee, and other states reveal that the editors of these papers are far from satisfied with the present disposition of the matter. Some of these editorials are about as strong in their disapproval as an editorial can be. . . ."[101]

As in past controversies of this nature, rectification was sought in the Southern Baptist Convention. Under the leadership of the Reverend K. Owen White, pastor of the First

[99] *Ibid.*
[100] Nashville *Baptist and Reflector*, Feb. 18, 1962.
[101] Kansas City *Word and Way*, Feb. 8, 1962.

Baptist Church of Houston, the dissidents mustered majority support in the 1962 convention at San Francisco. Delegates adopted one resolution emphatically affirming their faith in "the *entire* Bible as the authoritative, authentic, infallible Word of God." Another expressed "our abiding and unchanging objection to the dissemination of theological views in any of our seminaries which would undermine such faith in the historical accuracy and doctrinal integrity of the Bible, and that we courteously request the trustees and administrative officers of our institutions and other agencies to take such steps as shall be necessary to remedy at once those situations where such views now threaten our historic position."[102] Thus did the convention service notice, as the Oklahoma City *Baptist Messenger* approvingly observed, "that it is going to keep on being what it has been—a fellowship of Bible-believing, Bible-loving people. . . ."[103]

With the position of the convention thus established, the Sunday School Board and the seminary—as agencies of the convention—could hardly refuse to conform. Nor did they. The Sunday School Board quickly announced that it would not authorize a second printing of Elliott's now out-of-print volume.[104] At an October meeting, the Midwestern board of trustees (including several newly appointed members) designated a committee to confer with Elliott. When he refused to give assurances that there would be no further publication of his book by any press, at least "at this time," the committee recommended that he be dismissed. The full board approved this recommendation by vote of 24 to 5.[105] The action was justified on the technical grounds of insubordination to administrative authority. But the more fundamental causes were not obscured.

---

[102] Southern Baptist Convention, *Annual, 1962* (Nashville, n.d.), 68.
[103] Oklahoma City *Baptist Messenger,* quoted in Kansas City *Word and Way,* July 12, 1962.
[104] Nashville *Baptist and Reflector,* Sept. 20, 1962.
[105] *Ibid.,* Oct. 25, Nov. 8, 1962.

Though Elliott's interpretations of Genesis were probably acceptable to few Southern Baptists, the actions against him drew wide protests nevertheless. The editor of the Georgia *Christian Index* blamed the convention's provocative resolutions on western extremists who were prone to "slap down any accused of being off center but without waiting to be sure of guilt."[106] The *Arkansas Baptist* thought "it was a strange order of business for a convention of Baptists, who have prided themselves across the centuries for their religious liberty, to attempt to put a theological strait jacket of conformity on everybody and to come dangerously near reviving the Dark Ages practice of burning books and persecuting Christians in the name of Christ."[107] The editor of the Virginia *Religious Herald* warned against "so circumscribing theology that the young people of your coming generation who are thinkers will have no respect for it whatsoever."[108] The Maryland State Baptist Convention pointedly expressed its "confidence and pride in our several theological seminaries." The North Carolina state convention begged Baptists to "manifest an attitude of trust toward our Christian teachers."[109] The 1963 Southern Baptist Convention rebuffed efforts by ultraconservatives to rephrase portions of a new convention Statement of Faith and Message (which superseded the one of 1925). But delegates elected the leader of the anti-Elliott faction, the Reverend K. Owen White, as president of the convention.[110]

The Baptists were ample witness that, in deeper realms of mind and spirit, the hold of a pristine past was still strong. For it was as keepers of old traditions, guardians of old truths, that they prospered and flourished.

---

[106] Quoted in Kansas City *Word and Way*, July 12, 1962.
[107] Quoted *ibid.*
[108] Quoted *ibid.*, Mar. 1, 1962.
[109] Baptist Convention of Maryland, *Minutes, 1962* (n.p., n.d.), 113; Baptist State Convention of North Carolina, *Annual, 1962* (n.p., n.d.), 172.
[110] Southern Baptist Convention, *Annual, 1963* (Nashville, n.d.), 63, 69.

8

SOUTHERN PROTESTANTISM AND THE SOUTH

Jt is perhaps worth stating the truism that southerners are after all Americans, that they belong to that broad cultural grouping which comprises Western Civilization, that their social patterns are more national and occidental than regional, and that conservative Protestantism is by no means a peculiarly southern or American manifestation. The general rules of kinship, mating, and incest which prevail among southerners prevail among hundreds of millions around the world. The basic ethical and spiritual ideals which they acknowledge are widely acknowledged; nor are distortions of these ideals peculiar to the South. With other Americans, southerners recite the Declaration of Independence, venerate the Founding Fathers, and observe the Fourth of July. Shoulder to shoulder with other Americans they bear arms against foreign enemies. With people of other regions and national-

159

ities, they espouse common causes, wage common fights, celebrate common victories, sustain common defeats, endure common frustrations, and worship a common deity.

Yet it is not in their broad conformity to American and occidental standards that southerners are chiefly regarded, but in their departures from them. An old familiar stanza nostalgically eulogizes the South as a peculiar land of cotton where old times are not forgotten. Other portrayals emphasize the quaint prevalence of faith and virtue, of gentle manners and gentle discourse, of extended familial attachments, of hospitality. Less laudatory stereotypes also abound: of calomel and quinine, of collard greens, hot biscuits, and pork chitterlings, of judicial debacles à la Dayton and Scottsboro. And now in anguished commentaries the South looms freshly as the setting where John F. Kennedy was struck down, and where Kennedy's accused assassin was curiously murdered before a national television audience.

Among historians of the South, the views of Ulrich B. Phillips were in an earlier generation especially influential. Extended growing seasons fostered the cultivation of tobacco, cotton, and other staples, Phillips reasoned, and the production of these crops, in turn, "promoted the plantation system, which brought the importation of negroes, which not only gave rise to chattel slavery but created a lasting race problem." And the latter he singled out as a great "central theme." Whether asserted "with the frenzy of a demagogue or maintained with a patrician's quietude," Phillips wrote, the determination to keep the South a white man's country "is the cardinal test of a Southerner and the central theme of Southern history."[1]

Few contemporary scholars portray the South as so much a product of the weather. And, though none deny the signifi-

[1] Ulrich B. Phillips, *Life and Labor in the Old South* (Boston, 1929), 3; "The Central Theme of Southern History," *American Historical Review,* XXXIV (Oct., 1928), 31.

cance of racial reactions, few regard a commitment to white supremacy as indispensable to southernism. Almost all stress the derivatives of a cotton- and tobacco-oriented economy, and of an all-pervading ruralism. In their essays in 1930, the twelve authors of *I'll Take My Stand* eloquently depicted the sentimental attachments of the population to soil and community.[2] Francis Butler Simkins has, among others, more recently emphasized such ties. Simkins is sure that the chief interest of contemporary southern urbanites is "to establish country estates where they can spend their mellowing years amid horses, chickens, and hogs."[3] On the other hand, most textbook writers dwell on drearier aspects of the southern rural setting as they prevailed early in this century—share-crop tenancy, the crop lien system, greedy furnishing merchants, and the like.

Two facts of experience and condition are especially vital to any analysis of the South. First there is the fact of the Civil War, the great lost cause, and of the Reconstruction which the victor imposed. From this harrowing ordeal many legends have derived—of pillage, rape, and oppression—legends freshly instilled from generation to generation. And, secondly, there is the fact of extreme and abject poverty which the South has experienced through most of the last century—extreme and abject by standards that obtained elsewhere in America. Indeed a sectional disparity in wealth of such proportions within one nation is unusual if not unique in Western Civilization. The South, then, has been a region with painful memories joined politically with other regions whose history has been until recent years little but an optimistic chronicle of victories and achievements. It has been an impoverished region in a nation of comparative plenty, a nation where the Horatio Alger myth was much recited. And it has been a region often

[2] Twelve Southerners, *I'll Take My Stand: The South and the Agrarian Tradition* (New York, 1930; Harper Torchbook, 1963).

[3] *The South: A Documentary History*, ed. Ina Woestemeyer Van Noppen (Princeton, 1958), x.

held up to reproof and disdain in a nation prone to celebrate its high moral purpose. These facts do much to explain the South and the southerner.[4]

The stamp of the region has borne heavily on the churches. The Southern Baptist Convention and the (Southern) Presbyterian Church in the United States remain yet separate and estranged from their northern counterparts. And though the Methodist schism formally ended in 1939, white southerners jealously guard their autonomy in the reunited denomination. The Southeastern Methodist Jurisdiction has hotly resisted further moves toward national assimilation and has exercised its prerogatives more fully than the other five major jurisdictions. Sectionalism has perhaps been perpetuated more explicitly in the southern churches than in any other institution. And the churches have probably reflected regional outlooks as much as any institution or agency. It is understandable that the sermons of southern clergymen have been heavily toned with homilies on the hopelessness of the human condition, and on the perversity of history. And, understandably, southern Protestants have not been easily excited by schemes for worldly betterment, knowing as they have known the frustrations of hope and the bitterness of despair. With urbanization proceeding slowly in the South, most southern congregations held fast to traditional modes long after worship fashions in the North were generally modernized. Ruralism has been peculiarly reflected in southern religious programs, in doctrinal emphasis, in style of leadership, and in numerous other ways. Summer revivals persisted not merely as religious observances, but also as festivals of social interchange held during the lull between the final plowing and the onset of harvest. The meeting season was a welcome release for a population denied many emotional outlets which only urban environments afforded.

[4] See C. Vann Woodward's magnificent discussion of these points in *Burden of Southern History*, 3–25.

The blight of poverty was until recent years much reflected in the physical surroundings wherein religious services were conducted. Benches on which rural worshipers sat seldom were fashioned either for beauty or for comfort. Light at night and heat in winter were alike poorly provided. Windows were usually unscreened and were often in a state of ill repair. Mosquitoes, flies, and wasps often flitted impiously from pew to pew. Privies were only occasionally afforded. Lack of resources hampered the theological preparation of ministers, the competent religious instruction of laymen, and general public education as well. By northern standards, religious leadership and response in the South were quaintly unsophisticated. Educational inadequacies were perhaps most pathetically manifest in the general reluctance to grapple intellectually with the challenges of modern science and scholarship. Only in very recent years has the peculiar regional disparity in wealth been significantly reduced.

Mencken at Dayton was by no means the first to note the exalted status of the clergyman in southern society. In the early decades of the century the preacher was noticed in almost any crowd; in almost any home he was an honored guest. For him the housewife spread her finest linens, prepared her choice foods, and displayed about her treasured trinkets of refinement. In all this of course simple piety was expressed. But it was to the person as much as to the office that deference was given. For it is certainly true that the southern clergy has included in its ranks many of the ablest leaders of the region —men of towering presence, of eloquent speech, of humor and understanding, and of profound religious commitment. As the century progressed, great problems of the age were increasingly relegated to scientists, engineers, and officers of state. But preachers in the South continued to exercise large roles of public leadership through the 1920's, and until now in some communities. Few southern boys joked about clergymen until in the armed services they learned to revel in the lore of military chaplains. There has not been in the century any demonstration of clerical leadership in the North of such proportions as was rendered by the southern clergy in the anti-evolution crusade and in the Presidential campaign of 1928.

It is surely true that in this century the concern of southern Protestants has been more narrowly confined to spiritual regeneration than that of Protestants in the North. But the contrast is one of degree. The southern churches have maintained heavy commitments to higher education, to hospitals, to orphanages, and to other humanitarian enterprises both in their region and abroad.[5] Protestant convocations in the South have rendered pronouncements on social issues in much the same tenor as northern Protestant groups; southern Protestant Sunday school literature often applies Christian teachings to social relations. And on many occasions southern clergymen have resorted to political action in support of good causes. Southern Protestantism has been generally less concerned about conditions of labor, racial injustice, and fair civil procedures than northern Protestantism, and almost surely more concerned about personal conduct, blue laws, prohibition, and unchristian influences in public schools. It is also probable that social issues have been agitated less frequently from pulpits in the South than in the North.

Of course the southern and northern churches have been affected by, and have reacted to, many of the same events, developments, and conditions. The impacts and ramifications of the Great Depression, of World War I and World War II, of new technology, of modern medicine, of altered intellectual and theological outlooks, were not and are not confined to any one region, nation, or continent. Most trends

[5] In the academic year 1962–63, in the eleven states of the ex-Confederacy plus Oklahoma and Kentucky, 171,567 out of 853,230 students enrolled in institutions of higher learning (excluding theological seminaries and Y.M.C.A. schools) were enrolled in church-related schools. (US Office of Education, *Educational Directory, 1962–63*, Pt. III, "Higher Education" [Washington, 1963], *passim*.)

in southern Protestantism have also been present in northern Protestantism, though often not simultaneously, often not in equal strength, and often not in like manner of manifestation. Hence the segregation of whites and Negroes into separate local congregations has been the pattern both in the North and in the South. Occasional exceptions to this pattern may have been more numerous in the North.[6] Certainly in the North the principle of all-white denominationalism was not proclaimed and applied by the major religious bodies as it was by the Methodists and Baptists in the South. Likewise, pleas for racial justice have not been lacking among southern Protestants in recent years, but such agitation is less clamorous and forthright than in the North. Nor was the agitation against Darwinism and the teaching of evolution heard only in the South, though the crusade was pressed with more vigor, concert, and success in the South than in other areas. The aggressive modernist and fundamentalist campaigns in the 1920's were national and international, but fundamentalism reigned triumphant in the southern churches as it did not in major religious denominations in the North. Antimilitarism ran strong both in the North and in the South in the interval between the two world wars; pacifism, however, was probably more widely professed among northern Protestants than among southern Protestants. National prohibition was a cause dear to the clergy in all regions, but ecclesiastical leadership in behalf of prohibition was most forcefully asserted in the South, in the campaign of 1928. And though neo-orthodoxy, ecumenism, and the social gospel movement have all made impacts on southern Protestantism, the impact in each case was apparently greater in the North.

[6] Liston Pope of the Yale Divinity School concluded in 1947 that "there is little difference between southern and non-southern white churches, on the whole, in the degree to which they have failed to incorporate Negroes. The segregation of Negro Protestants into separate churches is practically universal throughout the country." (Liston Pope, "Caste in the Church: The Protestant Experience," *Survey Graphic,* XXXVI [Jan. 1947], 59, quoted in Culver, *Negro Segregation in The Methodist Church,* 9–10.)

Involvements and reactions become increasingly national and international as the century wears on. The South and the southern churches are being brought into closer association with the rest of the nation as the nation moves into closer association with the rest of the world, and the world into closer association with other planets. Sectionalism can hardly flourish in the future as it did in the past, or even as it does in the present. For as is the case with contrasts of nationality, religious faith, social class and family contrasts of region also grow less distinct.

Neither the South nor the world is much what it was at the outset of the century. Science and technology have advanced as if through a millennium. Paved highways crisscross where dusty roads and cowpaths once ran. Transportation and communication, work and play, education and child rearing, all are drastically different. In an age of diminishing regional identities, the South is wavering in its fidelity to the Democratic party. Its unusual poverty also wanes, as does its rurality and agrarianism, and even the distinctive speech of its people.

There is, however, some greater constancy in mind and spirit. A century of extraordinary adversity has well impressed upon southerners (and they will not soon forget) that good causes do not always prevail, that evil is not easily overcome, that wrongs are not inevitably righted, that hazards lurk always near at hand. Elation is seldom untempered by a consciousness of frailty and by memories of failures in the past. Nor do nuclear fission and intercontinental rockets enhance expectations of futurity in the South or elsewhere.

Religious faith remains conspicuous, though surely less conspicuous than at the first of the century. Churches of Christ and many smaller fundamentalist sects report large gains in recent decades. Old-time evangelism and a continuing commitment to Scriptural literalism also apparently do much to account for the Baptist upsurge. Long established as the most numerous religious group in the South, the Southern Baptists have recently emerged as the largest single Protestant denomination in America.[7]

Belief in progress has dimmed over the world, and gloom more than hope seems now to pervade our national temper. But southerners—more than other Americans generally—have before perceived the enormity of the human predicament and the inadequacies of their efforts to improve it. How often before, in anguish of spirit, they have prayed for remission and strength! And their doubtings have been calmed, their commitments renewed, their will and purpose reaffirmed.

[7] Southern Baptist Convention tabulations of membership in congregations affiliated with it in 1962 showed that 8,944,812 out of an aggregate of 10,193,-052 members resided in the eleven states of the ex-Confederacy plus Oklahoma and Kentucky. (*Southern Baptist Handbook, 1963* [Nashville, 1963], *passim.*)

A Bibliographical Essay

$\mathcal{A}$ general knowledge of the South is vital to an understanding of religion in the region. Hence the serious student is directed to the series edited by Wendell H. Stephenson and E. Merton Coulter, A History of the South (10 vols., Baton Rouge, La., 1948–). Volume IX, C. Vann Woodward's Origins of the New South, 1877–1913 (Baton Rouge, La., 1951), is a model in analysis and interpretation, and it contains an excellent bibliography; Volume X, being written by George B. Tindall and scheduled for publication in 1965, will cover the period from 1913 through 1946. Three good one-volume surveys are John S. Ezell, The South Since 1865 (New York, 1963), William B. Hesseltine and David L. Smiley, The South in American History (Englewood Cliffs, N. J., 1960), and Francis B. Simkins, A History of the South (New York, 1958). Thomas D. Clark's The Emerging South (New York, 1961) deals with the period since 1920, with special emphasis on economic development. An economist's analysis is given in William H. Nicholl's Southern Tradition and Regional Progress (Chapel Hill, 1960). The best study of regional political

169

behavior is V. O. Key, *Southern Politics in State and Nation* (New York, 1949); more recent political analyses are given in four of the nine essays in *Change in the Contemporary South,* ed. Allan P. Sindler (Durham, N. C., 1963). C. Vann Woodward's *Tom Watson: Agrarian Rebel* (New York, 1938) affords many insights on politics and race relations in the early twentieth century, as do Albert D. Kirwan's *Revolt of the Rednecks: Mississippi Politics, 1876–1925* (Lexington, Ky., 1951), and Dewey W. Grantham's *Hoke Smith and the Politics of the New South* (Baton Rouge, La., 1958). Twelve talented authors gave a classic defense of regional traditions in *I'll Take My Stand* (New York, 1930). Among other perceptive interpretations by native sons are: *The Lasting South: Fourteen Southerners Look at Their Past,* ed. Louis D. Rubin, Jr., and James J. Kilpatrick (Chicago, 1957), Ralph McGill, *The South and the Southerner* (Boston, 1963), Wilbur J. Cash, *The Mind of the South* (New York, 1941), *The Southerner as American,* ed. Charles G. Sellers, Jr. (Chapel Hill, 1960), and Harry Ashmore, *An Epitaph of Dixie* (New York, 1958). Regionalism and the regional character are treated succinctly in C. Vann Woodward, *The Burden of Southern History* (Baton Rouge, La., 1960), Francis B. Simkins, "The South," in *Regionalism in America,* ed. Merrill Jensen (Madison, Wis., 1954), 147–72, and in "The Status and Future of Regionalism—A Symposium," in *Journal of Southern History,* XXVI (Feb. 1960), 22–56.

Nor can Protestantism in the South be adequately comprehended without reference to national and international trends in religion. As a comprehensive treatment of American religion —historical and contemporary—*Religion in American Life,* ed. James W. Smith and A. Leland Jamison (4 vols., Princeton, 1961–63), will almost surely become a classic; the fourth volume is bibliographical, with extensive listings on almost every conceivable religious topic. Summaries of current issues by eleven eminent authors appear in *Religion in America,* ed. John Cogley (Cleveland, 1958). Perhaps the most satisfactory one-volume survey is that of Clifton E. Olmstead, *Religion in America: Past and Present* (Englewood Cliffs, N. J., 1961). Winthrop S. Hudson's *American Protestantism* (Chicago, 1961) is a more abbreviated interpretation designed also for general readers. Willard L. Sperry,

Religion in America (New York, 1946) was prepared for a British audience. Other scholarly volumes of interest to lay as well as clerical readers include: Herbert W. Schneider, *Religion in 20th Century America* (Cambridge, 1952), *Protestant Thought in the Twentieth Century*, ed. Arnold S. Nash (New York, 1951), Aaron I. Abell, *The Urban Impact on American Protestantism* (Cambridge, 1943), Henry F. May, *Protestant Churches and Industrial America* (New York, 1949), Charles H. Hopkins, *The Rise of the Social Gospel in American Protestantism, 1865–1915* (New Haven, 1940), Paul A. Carter, *The Decline and Revival of the Social Gospel, 1920–1940* (Ithaca, 1954), Robert Moats Miller, *American Protestantism and Social Issues, 1919–1939* (Chapel Hill, 1958), Donald B. Meyer, *The Protestant Search for Political Realism, 1919–1941* (Berkeley, 1960), Norman F. Furniss, *The Fundamentalist Controversy, 1918–1930* (New Haven, 1954), and Louis Gasper, *The Fundamentalist Movement* (The Hague, 1962). H. Richard Niebuhr's *The Kingdom of God in America* (Chicago, 1937) and Reinhold Niebuhr's *Essays in Applied Christianity* (New York, 1959) are two good selections from the many contributions of these noted brothers.

There is no better introduction to the study of southern religion than the essay by Edwin McNeill Poteat, Jr., "Religion in the South," in *Culture in the South*, ed. W. T. Couch (Chapel Hill, 1934), 248–69. Edmund deS. Brunner's *Church Life in the Rural South* (New York, 1923) and Victor I. Masters's *Country Church in the South* (Atlanta, 1913) are sociological in approach, as are Gordon W. Blackwell, *et al.*, *Church and Community in the South* (Richmond, 1949), and Liston Pope, *Millhands and Preachers: A Study of Gastonia* (New Haven, 1942). Of greater interest to the historian and the general reader is Hunter D. Farish, *The Circuit Rider Dismounts: A Social History of Southern Methodism, 1865–1900* (Richmond, 1938). A parallel study of equal merit—not yet in print—is Rufus B. Spain's "Attitudes and Reactions of Southern Baptists to Certain Problems of Society, 1865–1900," doctoral dissertation, Vanderbilt University, 1961. William W. Barnes's *The Southern Baptist Convention, 1845–1953* (Nashville, 1954) is an extensive treatment, useful as a reference tool. Robert G. Torbet, *A History of the Baptists* (Chicago, 1963) gives a competent survey of Baptists in the South and elsewhere. Methodism in the South and in the nation receives a thorough analysis—historical and contemporary—in *Methodism and Society*, ed. The Board of Social and Economic Relations of The Methodist Church (4 vols., Nashville, 1960–62). Ernest Trice Thompson's *Presbyterians in the South* (2 vols., Richmond, 1963–   ) gives promise of becoming the standard history of his denomination; Volume II, covering the period from 1861 to present, is expected to be published soon. Walter L. Lingle, *Presbyterians: Their History and Beliefs* (Richmond, 1950) is a good handbook. One of the more rewarding personal narratives by a recent southern Protestant leader is William O. Carver's *Out of His Treasure* (Nashville, 1956); Carver was a long-time professor at the Southern Baptist Theological Seminary. Among other useful biographies, reminiscences, and autobiographies of southern religious leaders are: Alfred M. Pierce, *Giant Against the Sky: The Life of Bishop Warren Akin Candler* (New York, 1948), John Miller Wells, *Southern Presbyterian Worthies* (Richmond, 1936), Powhatan W. James, *George W. Truett, A Biography* (Nashville, 1953), Virginius Dabney, *Dry Messiah: The Life of Bishop Cannon* (New York, 1949), and Isla May Mullins, *Edgar Young Mullins: An Intimate Biography* (Nashville, 1929). Washington Bryan Crumpton told of his labors as president of the Anti-Saloon League in Alabama and as corresponding secretary of the state Baptist Mission Board in *A Book of Memories, 1842–1920* (Montgomery, Ala., 1921). James Sellers, a divinity school professor at Vanderbilt University, rendered a probing analysis, with emphasis on the segregation crisis, in his *The South and Christian Ethics* (New York, 1962). And two Southern Baptists—Brooks Hays and John E. Steely—have recently collaborated in an excellent interpretation of *The Baptist Way of Life* (Englewood Cliffs, N. J., 1963).

INDEX

173

Bailey notes social procurement
of termination (41), but bold
implementation is lacking (43)

ministerial education
    requirements 54

liberal ala Bapt examis attitude 114
intransigent S B C 123 ff   116
sermons unrelated to living 133